THE FAITH OF A METHODIST

The Fernley-Hartley Lecture 1958
A Synopsis of which was delivered at
Elswick Road Methodist Church
Newcastle-upon-Tyne
on 9th July 1958

THE FAITH OF A METHODIST

by

ERIC BAKER

ABINGDON PRESS

NEW YORK   NASHVILLE

FIRST PUBLISHED IN 1958

Reprinted 1958
Reprinted 1959
Reprinted 1961
Reprinted 1964

© THE EPWORTH PRESS 1958

Book Steward
FRANK H. CUMBERS

REPRINTED PHOTO LITHO BY
EBENEZER BAYLIS AND SON, LTD.
THE TRINITY PRESS, WORCESTER, AND LONDON

TO

THE PEOPLE CALLED METHODISTS

IN GRATITUDE AND AFFECTION

PREFACE

WHEN the Fernley-Hartley Trustees honoured me by the invitation to deliver the 1958 Fernley-Hartley Lecture, I soon realized that it would be beyond my powers in the time available to undertake the necessary research involved in producing a book which would take its place as a contribution to scholarship such as has been made by many of my predecessors.

It occurred to me, however, that there might be room in the series for an altogether different kind of book with the average Methodist in mind rather than the scholar or the trained theologian. The Trustees readily agreed and I am grateful to them for their consideration and encouragement.

The book, as those who read it will discover, has its origin in a deep concern. It makes no pretence to originality and, while the opinions expressed are my own, anything of value it contains has been received from those who in conversation and in their writings have contributed to such understanding as I have of the faith of a Methodist.

ERIC BAKER

CONTENTS

Part I. An Argument

Part II. A Doctrinal Examination

Part I. An Argument

CHAPTER I

THE CHANGING SCENE

THIS book is written by a Methodist and for Methodists. If some who belong to other Christian Communions, or to none, should chance to scan its pages, it is hoped that they will do so with understanding and charity. One of the best-known and most often quoted sayings of John Wesley, the founder of Methodism, was that in which he described the Methodists as 'the friends of all and the enemies of none', and it is certainly in that spirit that these chapters are penned. 'Denominationalism is doomed', declared the late Dr Scott Lidgett not long before his death, and his words echo today in the hearts and consciences of countless Christians in the various Churches as they seek the way to heal their divisions and draw closer to one another. The task is urgent, for the world is perishing and needs the message which only the Church of Jesus Christ can proclaim, but which the Church can only proclaim with full effectiveness when it can speak with a united voice.

This is so not only because the message of a Church which speaks with many different voices will almost certainly appear confused, but even more because the message is one of reconciliation, first of man to God and then of man to his brother man, and a Church which is itself rent asunder by quarrels and disagreements it has so far failed to resolve can scarcely hope to prove an effective instrument for bringing to a torn and distracted world the unity it so sorely needs for its well-being, and, it may well be, for its very survival.

In this respect, a tremendous change has come over the ecclesiastical scene in the last fifty years. The first nineteen hundred years of Christian history were years of schism. I do not need to recall the details of the story. We are all aware of the great division between the Churches of the East and the West, of the Reformation, of the smaller divisions whose name is legion, of the birth and growth of Methodism and the schisms we have known within our group. But what a transformation we have witnessed in the last fifty years! When we are intimately concerned with these matters, progress often seems woefully slow, but let us take a glance over the last half-century. Within our own Methodist family in this country and elsewhere there has been a drawing together. But we are by no means alone in this. Think of Canada; think of Scotland where the Presbyterians have sunk their differences and brought into being that great Church of Scotland; think of South India where a union has taken place of special significance because the Anglicans, who have their own particular difficulties in these matters, have found it possible to play their part; think of North India, Ceylon, Pakistan, in each of which territories projects for union are at an advanced stage—and all in fifty years.

Side by side with these events there has been developing the ecumenical movement, the world-wide movement embodying Christians from all over the inhabited earth. Most people date the real beginning of that from the Edinburgh Conference of 1910, less than fifty years ago. In spite of the interruption of two world wars, and one of the worst effects of war is what it does to the preaching of the Gospel, the movement progressed so rapidly that in 1948 the first assembly of the World Council of Churches took place in Amsterdam. The most significant of the pronouncements of those delegates, representing more than one hundred and fifty Protestant and Orthodox

Communions, was that having come together they intended to stay together, and the second assembly was held at Evanston in 1954. The business of the ecumenical movement is not to promote Church union. It may help to do that, as a by-product, but its function is to provide a perpetual field of encounter, using that word in its best sense, whereby Christian corporate thinking may be stimulated and Christian co-operative action carried on in the many fields, such as inter-Church aid and service to refugees, where such practical action to meet human need is urgently called for.

Where do we look if we would see a gleam of hope in the desperate situation of the world today? To Moscow? Assuredly not, we should all agree. But not to London or Washington either, nor to the United Nations. This is not said in disparagement of statesmen or economists, whose ingenuity and help are indeed essential. But they have not the answer to the dilemma of today. We must rather look to Amsterdam and Evanston. The World Council of Churches is a frail and tender plant, and it has its share of growing pains; but there is hope there, because it is based upon reality. When we survey humanity today, the characteristic which is most distressingly apparent is mankind's diversity. Men are grouped together in opposing camps, nation against nation, class against class. At every point we are faced with conflicts of interest and motive. To resolve such conflicts seems completely beyond the power and ingenuity of statesmen. Such diversity, however, is not the last word. Deeper than mankind's diversity is its unity, a unity which might be all the richer because of the different elements of which it is composed. It is, however, only at the deepest level, the spiritual, that such unity is a fact. Its principle is not hidden or unknown. It has been made known and the Church exists to make it real. Men are one because God made them all and Jesus died for all. The hope for the world lies not so much in the conferences of statesmen, who are concerned more with the relatively superficial issues of politics and economics, but in the emergence of a World Church, which shall unite British and German, Chinese and Japanese, black and white, capitalist and socialist, in the family of the redeemed. In principle, this universality of Christendom was demonstrated among the first generation of Christians. While Christians were but a handful in a pagan world, they included Jew and Gentile, Greek and barbarian, slave and free, male and female. All the traditional barriers separating man from his brother man were broken down, and men were one in Christ Jesus. The racial barrier, the economic barrier, the most subtle division of all, that of sex, on which the whole social fabric rests, are all done away. This unity still awaits its full expression. But the World Church exists, as no other human institution exists, to give expression to that fundamental unity of mankind as children of God which underlies our diversity.

At the outset of this confession of faith, therefore, I affirm my belief in and allegiance to the World Church of Jesus Christ, wherein alone is hope for the world. It is in that context that all that is written here about Methodism should be considered. I believe in the Holy Catholic Church. In that regard, I am in complete harmony with the Deed of Union adopted by the Uniting Conference of the three Methodist Communions which came together in 1932 to form the Methodist Church of Great Britain. This contains the declaration: 'The Methodist Church claims and cherishes its place in the Holy Catholic Church which is the Body of Christ.'

In the light of this, some may ask, 'Why a book entitled *The Faith of a Methodist*?' If the things which unite all Christians are more important than the things which divide us, a proposition to which most of us would subscribe, is it profitable to stress the things which belong to a denomination? Would it not be better discreetly to shelve these and concentrate on those aspects of Christian truth that are common to all? I appreciate the point, but I profoundly disagree.

A friend of mine in the first World War, when presented with an enlistment form to be filled in, entered in the space opposite 'Religion' the word 'Christian'. It caused confusion amounting almost to consternation at the local recruiting office, and they brought him the form to amend. 'But I don't wish to alter it,' he protested. 'It is as a Christian I desire to be entered.' 'But it's impossible,' came the reply, 'we haven't got that category! You must put "C. of E." or "R.C." or "Wesleyan".'

The authorities were right. It was true then, as it remains true today, that anyone desiring to be a member of the Church of Jesus Christ can only do so by becoming a member of one of the various Christian denominations. If a man refuses this but still insists on his right to be a Christian, he has in effect taken the first step toward founding a new denomination—which is hardly the way forward at the present time.

Moreover, if it be true, as the events of the last fifty years would suggest, that the Holy Spirit is leading the scattered members of Christ's Body into closer association, it is of the utmost importance that every denomination should enter that new association with its flags flying. I can think of nothing more disastrous than that the various Protestant Churches should shed the distinctive elements in their traditions and become merged into a kind of amorphous mass. On the contrary, the best service anyone can render at the present time to the Holy Universal Church of Jesus Christ is to be the best possible Methodist or Anglican or Quaker or whatever it may be. We must enter any new relationships into which God may call us bringing gladly such aspects of truth as the Holy Spirit may appear to have committed especially to us, and at the

same time being humbly willing to have our store enlarged by what other traditions than our own may
possess. Otherwise the result of any coming together would
be impoverishing when it should be enriching.

Not long ago a dear old lady belonging to another
Communion, on learning to her regret that I did not belong to her Church but was a Methodist, remarked:
'Oh well, it doesn't really matter; we are all going to the
same place in the end.' She meant it kindly, though I
never learned how she had made that discovery. But her
remark was typical of an attitude, prevalent among many,
which I believe to be profoundly mistaken. For the time
being, denominations do matter, and the idea that our
differences are only concerned with secondary matters of
organization, and that a Christian should be able to move
from one Communion to another and hardly notice it,
is quite wrong. Fundamentally, of course, we are all
Christians, worshipping the same Lord, but our divisions
did not come about accidentally, nor are they meaningless. New denominations did not come into being
merely because those who founded them thought there
were not enough already. Furthermore, though it seems
clear that our Lord Himself willed that His followers
should be one, and, in consequence, we recognize the sin
of disunity, few of us would wish to deny that actions
which have led to schism have often been taken because,
in the existing state of affairs, no alternative seemed
possible if vital truths were to be witnessed to and
defended, and the Gospel faithfully proclaimed. Certainly, we Methodists, contemplating our own beginnings,
would make that claim. Historically regarded, our denominational differences are not wholly sinful, though their
perpetuation may be in the new situation facing us today.

When through marriage with someone of another
Communion, or perhaps through moving to a new area
where his own Communion has no church, a Christian

changes his denomination, we may rejoice in that recognition of our fundamental oneness in Christ which makes the change possible and maybe even enriching, but, while admitting that no change in personal allegiance to our Lord need be involved, let us not pretend that there has been no significant change in churchmanship.

So I believe that it means something quite definite to be a Methodist and not some other sort of Christian. If a notice-board announces that the church outside which it stands is a Methodist church, a visitor has a right to expect that the sermon he will hear inside will be different from what he will hear in any of the neighbouring churches, and quite often, though not invariably, his expectation will be realized. He has a right to expect that some different hymns will be sung, and almost certainly that will happen. And if he participates in the week-day activities of the community at that church, they too will have a characteristically Methodist flavour that he will not find elsewhere.

For we Methodists have a distinctive ethos all our own. We are the youngest of the great Protestant Communions. It is only a little over two hundred years since Methodism began, and though that would be a very long time in the life of an individual, it is a very short time for a Church. When we started, all the other great Christian Communions were well established. Yet God so blessed John Wesley and the early Methodist preachers, and has continued so to bless their successors, that in this comparatively short space of time Methodism has become a great world Church, to which the Holy Spirit seems to have committed many treasures, not only for our own building up in the faith, but to be held in trust for the Universal Church of Jesus Christ.

We Methodists have much to learn from our fellow-Christians and some things to teach, and it is with one of those latter things that I am especially concerned in this book.

CHAPTER II

METHODISM AND THEOLOGY

IT is a salutary experience to be present and listen to what our friends in other Communions say about Methodism on those occasions when we meet on common platforms and compliments are exchanged. Frequently they pay tribute to our genius for organization, which seems to be the envy of others, if sometimes it is our own despair. They may refer to our evangelical zeal and the spiritual leadership we expect and so often receive from our laymen. Almost certainly they will make reference to the warmheartedness which traditionally characterizes our churchmanship. One fact about Methodism that everybody seems to be aware of is that it all began on 24th May 1738 at a quarter to nine in the evening when the heart of John Wesley was 'strangely warmed'. We, too, must continually thank God on every remembrance of that event, without which Methodism, as we know it, would never have come into existence. Warm hearts let us hope we shall always have, but I have an uncomfortable feeling that sometimes in the minds of our friends these warm hearts are accompanied by weak heads, although they are far too polite to say so. Be that as it may, I have never on any single occasion heard our ability to grasp and present the great truths of the Christian Gospel singled out for comment. The plain fact is that, while it is generally recognized that Methodism's contribution to the universal Church is many-sided, it is not usually regarded as being to any great extent in the field of theology. This is probably due, in no small part, to the unwillingness of John Wesley to impose any doctrinal test as a condition of entrance to the Methodist Society. Two quotations, separated in their utterance by a period of no less than forty-six years, will suffice to illustrate this. In 1742 he wrote: 'The distinguishing marks of a Methodist are not his opinions of any sort.' In 1788 he declared: 'There is no other religious society under heaven which requires nothing of men in order to their admission into it but a desire to save their souls. . . . The Methodists alone do not insist on your holding this or that opinion, but they think and let think.' After two centuries the same is true throughout what has during that period become perhaps the largest Protestant Church in the world.

To deduce from this, however, as some do, that John Wesley was indifferent to theological truth is to be guilty of a profound error, of which even a superficial knowledge of his writings or of Charles Wesley's hymns will suffice to disabuse us. It is one thing to regard theological orthodoxy as an unsuitable test of Church membership, but a very different thing to count it of little importance. But it must be confessed that the average Methodist tends to regard theology as an academic subject only to be studied by specialists. Ministers, it is recognized, ought to know something about it, although it is to be hoped that they won't let the fact be too evident in their sermons. A few scholars should become expert in it so that they can teach students in college as much as they need to know, though even the colleges should devote more time, it is urged, to what are deemed practical subjects, and so fit the young minister for the many-sided work which awaits him in the Circuits.

All this is the most arrant nonsense, and it would be summarily dismissed in any other field of human activity. Nothing matters so much as what a man believes. It determines in the end how he behaves and what kind of man he becomes. Behind all sound practice is sound theory. Would society tolerate doctors who had not passed their tests in anatomy, physiology, etc.? It is true that in the exercise of his practice a doctor gains invaluable experience, but a sound training in the theory is an essential foundation. Theology simply means what we believe about God. If a man's belief is the most important thing about him, what he believes about God is the most important part of his belief. It only needs a little reflection to show that the root of all the distresses which afflict men and nations is unbelief. A restoration of vital belief in God, His nature, will and purpose, is the prime need of the age.

Furthermore, when we turn to Methodism, we discover that all our practical genius and our emphasis on experience is rooted in belief and springs directly from it. It is often remarked that John Wesley was not a theologian, and sometimes those who make the observation do so as if they thought they were paying him a compliment. But the observation is simply not true, and would suggest that those who make such an astonishing assertion have confined their reading of his voluminous writings to the various grammars and the monograph on *Primitive Physick*. Everything else is theology and theology and again theology. Open one of the volumes of his *Letters* at any page and it is not possible to read many lines before coming across a statement that springs right out of his belief. If this be pointed out, it will probably draw the rejoinder that what was meant was that John Wesley was not an original theologian. In other words, he didn't invent his theology. That is true and we may rejoice in it. Wesley had no theology but what he found in Scripture, but there is an originality of emphasis which is as authentic as an originality of invention. In this respect John Wesley was one of the great theologians of all time. He did something which, as far as I am aware, had never been done since the earliest days of the faith, and as a result of it he left behind him a movement which not only bears in its remarkable organization the impress of his practical genius, but is also entrusted with a presentation of the Christian faith, based indeed at every point on Holy Scripture but in emphasis peculiarly its own, not only in the eighteenth century, when it swept England like a prairie fire, but also to this present day. That is why, as stated above, the sermons preached and the hymns sung in a Methodist church may be expected to be different from, though not contrary to, those encountered elsewhere.

Wherein does this peculiar emphasis lie? Chiefly, I would maintain, in the stress continually placed by Wesley on the Doctrine of Christian Perfection. There is of course also the Doctrine of Assurance which equally with the Doctrine of Christian Perfection forms a distinctive part of our Methodist tradition. 'The Spirit Himself', wrote St Paul, 'beareth witness with our spirit that we are children of God.' That is to say, a man may not only be saved through faith in Jesus Christ but he may know that he is saved, and this exultant assurance should be the normal experience of all who, through repentance, accept the offer of salvation and are themselves accepted by God. That is the joyful experience of which Charles Wesley wrote in such hymns as:

> *My God, I am Thine;*
> *What a comfort divine,*
> *What a blessing to* know *that my Jesus is mine!*

Such an experience, however, while characteristic of authentic Methodism throughout its history belongs essentially to the realm of the feelings rather than that of the mind or the will. It is something bestowed by God and to be accepted by the believer rather than analysed or directly sought. It varies in intensity with different people and with the same people at different times, and its presence at any particular moment should never be regarded as a test of the validity of a man's faith or his acceptance by God. Otherwise sincere and devoted Christians can be tormented even to the point of despair because they seem to lack some feeling they think they ought to have which cannot be induced to order but which God in His wisdom bestows or withholds as seems good to Him. In rather a similar way, many people make quite unnecessary difficulties for themselves about prayer, and sometimes even go to the length of abandoning it because, when they pray, they do not seem to enjoy feelings of a particular kind which they have for some reason or other assumed should almost automatically be engendered by the act of prayer. But neither the reality nor the efficacy of prayer depends on feelings.

It is not, therefore, with Assurance but with the Doctrine of Christian Perfection, which colours Wesley's whole interpretation of the Gospel, that this book is concerned. First of all, it should be noticed how John Wesley's own spiritual history was responsible for his teaching on this matter. Methodism was born on 24th May 1738, when John Wesley experienced his evangelical conversion. But that was in fact Wesley's second conversion. Thirteen years before, in 1725, as a result of reading the works of Jeremy Taylor, Thomas à Kempis, and especially William Law, Wesley had undergone a moral conversion, as a result of which he explicitly resolved to be 'all devoted to God in body, mind, and spirit'. He then 'made a decision', as Dr Rattenbury says, 'from which he never deviated and which determined the whole course of his career'. For the next thirteen years, which included the period of his mission to Georgia, he strove by every means in his power to be good, but all in vain. It was for him a time of spiritual frustration. Then in 1738 came the evangelical conversion, which was not the conversion of a bad man, as commonly understood, into a good man, but the conversion of a good man into a Christian. Wesley now experienced the transforming power of God in his heart, as a result of which what had been only an impossible ideal became a joyous reality. From then on Wesley proclaimed, and bade his followers proclaim, Christian perfection as God's offer to every believer through faith in Jesus Christ. It should be noted, however, that he never claimed to have received it himself.

All this is made clear again and again in his voluminous writings. 'All our preachers', he says, 'should make a point of preaching perfection to believers constantly, strongly and explicitly, and all believers should mind this one thing and continually agonize for it.' In his own account of Christian perfection, revised and enlarged in 1777, he refers to the great sermon on 'the circumcision of the heart', in which he expounded the doctrine before the University of Oxford in 1733, five years before the evangelical conversion, and remarks: 'This was the view of religion I then had, which even then I scrupled not to call "perfection". This is the view I have of it now without any material addition or diminution.' In September 1790 he wrote: 'This doctrine is the grand depositum which God has lodged with the people called Methodists; and for the sake of propagating this chiefly He appears to have raised us up.' Two months later, and only a few weeks before his death, he wrote: 'If we can prove that any of our Local Preachers or Leaders, either directly or indirectly, speak against it, let him be a Local Preacher or Leader no longer. I doubt whether he shall continue in the Society. Because he that can speak thus in our congregations cannot be an honest man.'

Wesley had several alternative names for Christian Perfection, such as Entire Sanctification, Scriptural Holiness, and Perfect Love, the last named being particularly important as denoting that the perfection we may look for is not of power, nor of knowledge, but of love.

Over the period of years there are inconsistencies which may be detected, and in one important aspect Wesley modified his view. He came to recognize that Christians can fall from grace, a view from which he at first dissented. His mature judgement on this point is recorded in the *Minutes of Conference* of 1770: 'Does not talking of a justified or a sanctified state tend to mislead men? Almost naturally leading them to trust in what was done in one moment? Whereas we are every hour and every minute pleasing or displeasing to God according to our works.'

It is no part of the intention of this book to offer a detailed and comprehensive exposition of the doctrine of Christian Perfection (indeed that has been done by others), but rather to demonstrate its centrality in our Methodist tradition. Let me add, therefore, that the evidence of John Wesley's writings, examples of which as given above could be multiplied, is abundantly confirmed by Charles Wesley's hymns. We will examine this in greater detail in the next chapter. At this point I would content myself with remarking that this emphasis on Christian Perfection not only dominated the theological outlook of the founders of Methodism but maintained its central place wherever Methodism extended its influence throughout the eighteenth and nineteenth centuries. The scene of Methodism's most impressive growth during this period was undoubtedly the United States of America where the familiar figure of the Circuit rider followed hard in the wake of the settlers as they trekked westward. So successful was the Methodist movement in America that it may fairly be claimed that Methodism is the nearest approach to an indigenous form of Christianity that great country possesses. Here is an extract from the address delivered at a centenary celebration in New York in 1866 by John McClintock, first President of Drew Theological Seminary:

Methodism takes the old theology of the Christian Church, but it takes one element which no other Christian Church has dared to put forward as a prominent feature of theology. In ours it is the very point from which we view all theology. Now listen; I want that to be understood. Knowing exactly what I say, and taking the full responsibility of it, I repeat, we are the only Church in history, from the apostles' time until now, that has put forward as its very elemental thought—the great central pervading idea of the whole Book of God from the beginning to the end—the holiness of the human soul, heart, mind, and will. Go through all the confessions of all the churches, and you will find this in no other. You will find even some of them that blame us in their books and writings. It may be called fanaticism, but, dear friends, that is our mission. If we keep to that, the next century is ours; if we keep to that, the triumphs of the next century shall throw those that are past far into the shade. Our work is a moral work—that is to say, the work of making men holy. Our preaching is for that, our church agencies are for that, our schools, colleges, universities, and theological seminaries are for that. There is our mission—there is our glory—there is our power, and there shall be the ground of our triumph. God keep us true.

CHAPTER III

THE SIGNIFICANT METHODIST DOCTRINE

IF we are to understand the unique place of this doctrine of Christian Perfection in our Methodist tradition, we must recognize at the start and keep in our minds throughout that the doctrine must never be held in isolation. This is the mistake made by those sects which, no doubt with genuine devotion and sincere intent, so stress personal inward holiness to the exclusion of all else that their expression of Christianity becomes distorted. Anyone who has attempted to commend the doctrine of Christian Perfection to our fellow Methodists in the United States knows what an initial obstacle has to be overcome because of the prevalence of such 'holiness' sects, and, though they do not usually go to such fantastic extremes, similar examples could be found in this country.

In fairness to these sects, it should be recognized that, in however inadequate and indeed mistaken a fashion, they have been genuinely striving to fill the vacuum created by the neglect of this doctrine by the major Christian denominations. A similar situation has arisen in recent times in relation to the doctrine of eternal life, where the failure of the Church to present the Christian teaching about the hereafter in a convincing manner has permitted the spiritualists to annex that sphere as their own preserve.

If the doctrine of Christian Perfection is to be properly appreciated and accorded its authentic significance, two safeguards are necessary. First, it must be given its place within the impressive structure of Christian theology, and second, it must constantly be related to the life of the world and find its expression in individual and corporate behaviour.

Consider the first of these conditions. Therein lies one difference between a Church and a sect. A sect confines itself to the cultivation of one aspect of Christian truth, often to the neglect of many others, with the result that its witness is at best incomplete and tends to become entirely unbalanced. A Church, while emphasizing some elements more than others, nevertheless seeks to proclaim the whole truth of the Gospel and welcomes into its ranks believers of every type who respond to the love of God in Jesus Christ and accept Him as Saviour and Lord.

Now our Methodist concern is not with the doctrine of Christian Perfection as some kind of appendage to or consequence of the Gospel, but as an integral element in it apart from which the whole Gospel cannot be preached. It is our conviction that the full range of evangelical truth includes not only God's forgiving grace but God's enabling grace. The first truth of the Gospel, we should all agree, is God's offer of free forgiveness to sinful men and women. God's mercy is infinite and there is a welcome home for the returning sinner, however far he may have wandered and however long he may have stayed away. That is where we must begin, but it is not where we end. Our response to God's invitation is what John Wesley, borrowing the metaphor from *The Pilgrim's Progress*, called the 'wicket-gate' of salvation. Heaven knows we all need forgiveness, but forgiveness, with all its wonder, is not enough. This is nowhere set forth more clearly than in the familiar couplet of a well-loved hymn:

> *He died that we might be forgiven;*
> *He died to make us good.*

The first of these lines contains the very foundation of our evangelical faith. We may not understand it—indeed, it is a great and glorious mystery—but we do recognize the connexion between the redemptive death of our Lord and the forgiveness of our sins. But how often in our thought we stop there, when we should go on: 'He died to make us good.' Not only forgiveness but goodness is the gift of God through Jesus Christ. So many people only seem to believe half the Gospel. They appear to think of God as wiping our dirty slates clean, in His mercy, and then returning them to us with the injunction now to write better on them. Small wonder the slates are soon as dirty as ever. The truth is that goodness, like forgiveness, is something we can neither earn nor buy, neither deserve nor acquire, by any effort of our own. It is the gift of God through Jesus Christ. It seems a strange thing that these two truths, as inseparable in the Gospel as the two sides of a penny, should ever have been sundered, but it has been so, and it was the genius of John Wesley to reunite them, and publish them to all the world as the twin pillars of evangelical truth. Here is how the late Dr George Croft Cell puts it in his stimulating book, *The Rediscovery of John Wesley—*

The most important fact therefore about the Wesleyan understanding of the Gospel in relation to the Christian ethic of life is that the early Protestant doctrine of justification by faith and the Catholic appreciation of the idea of holiness or Christian perfection—two principles that had been fatally put asunder in the great Church conflicts of the sixteenth century—reappeared in the comprehensive spirit of Wesley's teaching.

In this judgement Dr Cell is reaffirming what Alexander Knox, Wesley's younger contemporary and follower, had declared many years before:

Never, elsewhere, except in the apostles themselves, and in the sacred books they have left, were the true foundation and the sublime superstructure of Christianity so effectively united.

No better evidence need be sought for the justice of this claim than that which is afforded by Charles Wesley's hymns. This is no place for an analysis of the thousands of hymns he wrote, nor is there need, since a study of those still current among us and included in our present hymn-book will provide ample illustration.

Best known among them are the evangelical hymns which deal with God's infinite mercy and forgiving grace. 'O for a thousand tongues to sing', 'And can it be that I should gain', 'Jesus, the name high over all', and 'What shall I do my God to love' are familiar examples. But if we turn to the section of the book entitled *Christian Holiness*, we find there twenty-eight hymns, all but six of which are by Charles Wesley. If it be said that most of these hymns are less well known than those cited above, I should agree and add that it is for that very reason that I am writing this book. We are in real danger of losing, through neglect, this precious heritage of ours, and that would be not only a disaster for Methodism but a betrayal of our sacred trust. But the point is that of these twenty-two hymns of Wesley only one, 'O for a heart to praise my God', is in common use outside our Church. Even those we Methodists sing frequently, such as 'Saviour, from sin I wait to prove' and 'God of all power and truth and grace'—this latter surely the greatest of them all, and one which I should like to feel most of us know by heart—are not included in any of the other well-known collections. But the expression of this doctrine in Charles Wesley's writings is by no means confined to hymns which, because it is their main theme, appear in this section. Turn to what section you will, it will be found that almost invariably perfectionist teaching is at any rate implicit and usually explicit. Time and time again a reference to it appears at the very end of a hymn on some quite different subject. Here are two or three examples taken almost at random. The hymn of dedication, 'My God, I know, I feel Thee mine', ends:

> Scatter Thy life through every part
> And sanctify the whole.

The hymn of Christian fellowship, 'Jesus we look to Thee', ends:

> And bid our inmost souls rejoice
> In hope of perfect love.

And the hymn of adoration and thanksgiving for the grace of the Lord Jesus Christ, 'Jesus comes with all His grace', ends:

> We shall gain our calling's prize,
> After God we all shall rise,
> Filled with joy and love and peace,
> Perfected in holiness.

These examples are by no means exceptional but rather typical of many that could have been chosen. Indeed, if the compiler of a hymn-book wished to include a representative selection of Charles Wesley's hymns, but wished on doctrinal grounds to exclude hymns where the doctrine of 'Christian Perfection' is stated or implied, he would be faced with a well-nigh impossible task, so fundamental is this truth to Wesley's whole understanding of the Gospel. One of its noblest expressions occurs in the concluding verse of 'Love divine, all loves excelling', a hymn sung in all the Churches, which no collection is likely to omit:

> Finish then Thy new creation,
>   Pure and spotless let us be;
> Let us see Thy great salvation,
>   Perfectly restored in Thee;
> Changed from glory into glory,
>   Till in heaven we take our place,
> Till we cast our crowns before Thee,
>   Lost in wonder, love, and praise.

We now turn to the other necessary safeguard mentioned above, namely the necessity of relating Christian Perfection to the life of the world. One of the greatest living philosophers has declared that 'all true life is meeting'. In other words, the meaning of life is realized through encounter. If we could imagine a new-born baby whisked away and deposited on a desert island, and if we could further imagine that in some extraordinary way the child did not perish but grew up into a man, he would only grow up physically; for the process of growing up spiritually depends on his recognition of and adjustment to other personalities—first of all to his mother and those in his intimate family group, and subsequently to others in an ever-widening circle. But the supreme encounter in which a man engages, and on which finally everything depends, is with his God. Perfect love is love to God and love to man. These are not separate but interdependent. 'He that loveth not his brother, whom he hath seen, cannot love God whom he hath not seen.' Similarly, John Wesley declared: 'There is no holiness but social holiness.' Holiness exists not in a vacuum but in right relationships. It becomes debased if it is divorced from practical expression, but in the true Methodist tradition theory and practice have gone together. This is how

Benjamin Hellier, a nineteenth-century Methodist theologian, expounded it:

Entire sanctification means the sanctification of everything. The sanctification, for example, of the daily work; that is, doing it to the Lord, and, therefore, doing it as well as we can. If a ploughman be entirely sanctified, he will plough a straight furrow—or at least try his best to do so. If he be a mason, he will put no bad work into his walls; if a doctor, he will care more about curing his patients than about getting large fees; if he be a minister of religion, he will strive to serve the people of his charge to the utmost of his ability. . . . Entire sanctification means dedicating all our property to God. When Christians ask themselves, 'How much of my money shall I devote to religious purposes?' they do not consider rightly. There ought to be no question of 'how much'; all must be devoted to God. . . . Entire sanctification means simply this: spending all our time in the Lord's service; making our religion our life, our life our religion.

What a contrast to the language used at some Holiness Conventions! Furthermore, this was characteristic of the practical and experimental religion of the early Methodists. The doctrine of holiness was hammered out in English kitchens and drawing-rooms where the early Methodists met for their weekly meetings. Week by week these folk encouraged one another by recounting the triumphs of God's grace in their everyday experience. 'The drunkard commenced to be sober and temperate; the whoremonger abstained from adultery and fornication; the unjust from oppression and wrong. He that had been accustomed to curse and swear for many years now swore no more. The sluggard began to work with his hands, that he might eat his own bread. The miser learned to deal his bread to the hungry, and to cover the naked with a garment.' Indeed the whole form of their life was changed. They had 'left off doing evil and learned to do well'.

The Christian perfection, then, with which we are concerned, far from being isolated from the doctrinal theory or the practical action of Christianity, is indispensable to them both, representing as it does the goal to which God's redemptive action in Jesus is both calling us and leading us, which goal is not separate from or outside our ordinary individual and corporate human concerns, but is one which, when attained, will be found to embrace them all.

CHAPTER IV

THE NEW TESTAMENT SOURCE

THERE can be no shadow of doubt as to the source of the doctrine of Christian Perfection preached by Wesley; he proclaimed it because in his view it was the clear and unmistakable teaching of the New Testament. When he was attacked on the point, as he often was, that was his invariable defence. 'What is there which any man of understanding, who believes the Bible, can object to? What can he deny, without contradicting the Scripture?' To this claim there would appear to be no reply. If we accept, as most New Testament scholars do, the general trustworthiness of the first three Gospels, it is unquestionable that Jesus Himself set forth perfection as the standard of behaviour for His disciples. 'Be ye perfect, even as your Father in heaven is perfect.' Everything else He enjoined can be regarded as commentary on this all-inclusive command. I have quoted the Authorized Version of the New Testament. In the Revised Version the command becomes a promise: 'Ye shall be perfect.' We shall never know which is the original of St Matthew, as the form of the Greek verb is the same. It is usually regrettable when we are left in doubt on a point of this kind, but in this instance there is no cause for regret. If it be a command, the command implies a promise, for assuredly this is not something within our powers apart from divine help. If it be a promise, then the promise implies a command. In the Christian life, the indicative and the imperative become one and the same. Perfection is the measure of God's demand because it is the measure of His offer. The Christian is freed from the requirements of any external code, but a much higher standard is put in its place.

In the above paragraph I have dealt with the text of the Sermon on the Mount at its face value as it appears in St Matthew's Gospel. Beyond all question that was also the way in which the Wesleys interpreted it. Those scholars may well be right who regard the form in St Luke as more likely to be the original, where the rendering 'merciful' appears instead of 'perfect'. But, of course, the teaching of our Lord on this matter does not depend on the authenticity of any single saying as a literal translation of His actual words, but on the cumulative evidence of His teaching as a whole, where the character of God is made the ground of human conduct and the highest external standard is rejected and the principle of love which knows no limits takes its place. Over and over again Jesus interprets that love as likeness to God; indeed the crucial words of the text which I have quoted are not really 'Be ye perfect' or 'Be ye merciful', but 'as your Father in heaven'. They carry the same teaching as other words of His, as when, for example, He said that men were like fellow-servants who ought to forgive one another because their heavenly Father had forgiven them, that they ought to be peace-makers because that was the way for them to be like (or to be 'sons of') God, that they ought to be glad when the prodigal returned home as God was glad, and that they ought to love their enemies because God was 'kind towards the unthankful and evil'. And since He and the Father are one, our Lord is saying the same thing when He tells men that they must be like Himself, that they must learn to be meek and lowly of heart as He was, and wash one another's feet because He had washed theirs, and love one another as He had loved them. Thus the whole tenor of the teaching of Jesus is that a love which is less than perfect is below what God requires. The only love which will ultimately satisfy Him is one like His own.

A great deal is being written today about the return to biblical theology, and many claims are made on its behalf. I would only plead that it should be a return to the theology of the Bible as a whole, in which event the teaching of our Lord would be accorded a more prominent place than appears to be the current fashion. In my opinion, nothing has been more disastrous to the Christian cause in recent years than the neglect of the teaching of Jesus, which should always have a primary place in our proclamation of the Gospel. Indeed, apart from it there is no Gospel. For what is the content of the salvation we offer to men in Christ's name? It begins, I need hardly say, with the offer of free forgiveness for our sins. There is nowhere else for it to begin. Unless men have a sense of need, the very offer of salvation will seem irrelevant. Perhaps the chief difficulty about preaching the Gospel today lies not in persuading men that God will forgive them, but in persuading them that they need His forgiveness. Every genuine evangelical experience must be preceded by a moral awakening, and one of the most disquieting features of contemporary life is the apparent absence of any widespread sense of moral need. Even at this point the teaching of Jesus has its part to play. Most of us can pass muster not only with the crowd around us but with Moses, too. 'Thou shalt not commit adultery.' 'Thou shalt do no murder.' These injunctions do not cause us to blush but when we are bidden, 'Love your enemies, and pray for them that persecute you', it is another story, and when we are brought face to face with Jesus not on the Galilean hillside where He taught the multitude but on that other hill, without a city wall, where He triumphantly passed His own test, our garb of respectability is stripped from us. It is then forgiveness that we need and forgiveness that He offers. But forgiveness is only the first of His gifts. What does forgiveness imply? Is it the remission of the just penalty we have incurred by our sins? That is a very superficial view. The penalty of sin is not some arbitrary and fearful punishment that is visited upon us by an angry God, but consists rather in what we ourselves become as a consequence of the separation from God that our sin brings about. Forgiveness means primarily our re-admission into fellowship with God and all that flows from that. Men are saved not from the consequence of their sins but from the sins themselves. They are saved both from something and into something. 'If they are converted at all,' wrote Wesley, 'they are converted from all manner of wickedness to a sober, righteous and godly life.' The real tragedy of much evangelistic effort in the last generation has been that what may well have been a genuine experience has all too often taken place in a vacuum, and in consequence has had no permanent effect. Some thirty years ago, on arriving in a new Circuit, I found in a drawer of the desk in the study a list containing hundreds of names. I was puzzled, because the names bore no relation to any of my other lists of Church members, Sunday-school scholars, etc. As no one seem⸗ able to offer any explanation, I wrote to my predecessor and inquired the significance of the list. The reply was that they were names of those who had signed decision cards during a campaign conducted the previous year by the most renowned evangelist of that day. The names were there, but that was the only remaining trace. The forgiving grace of God may well have been experienced on the occasion of their professed conversion; that we are in no position to affirm or deny. But of moral renewal, issuing in reformed lives and manifesting the fruits of the Spirit there was no evidence. A similar disappointing result would appear to be characteristic of much evangelistic enterprise still. Such experiences, so limited in their effects, fall far short of the full salvation offered by the

Christian Gospel. Forgiveness is the first, but only the first, of God's gifts to us in the Gospel. It should mark the beginning of God's gracious activity in the human soul which will know no end until He has transformed us into the people He intends us to become.

If this is true, it means that the teaching of Jesus must be restored in our thinking as well as in our preaching to the central position from which it should never have been displaced. We must recognize that the view which seeks to exalt Jesus the Saviour at the expense of Jesus the Teacher is not only unscriptural and untrue but a view which ultimately defeats its own end, as it empties the salvation it proclaims of the moral content with which it is supremely concerned.

Nor should it be thought that the teaching of Jesus stands by itself in this respect in the New Testament. The Gospels in their present form are among the later writings of the New Testament. The earliest books are the epistles of St Paul, who was not only the first great Christian missionary but who also plunged into virgin forests of thought and set forth the doctrine of our redemption in a form which has proved determinative for Christian theology to the present day. How does St Paul describe again and again what is to be the end of our salvation? Here, for example, he writes in the heyday of his ministry to the young Church at Corinth: 'We all, with unveiled face, reflecting as a mirror the glory of the Lord, are transformed into the same image from glory to glory, even as from the Lord the Spirit.' Or later, writing during his imprisonment at Rome towards the end of his life, he addresses the Church at Colossae: 'And you, being in time past alienated and enemies in your mind in your evil works, yet now hath he reconciled in the body of his flesh through death, to present you holy and without blemish and unreproveable before him: if so be that ye continue in the faith, grounded and stedfast, and not moved away from the hope of the gospel which ye heard, which was preached in all creation under heaven.' We must remember, too, another New Testament writer. A generation later in 1 John 3[2] we read, 'Beloved, now are we children of God, and it is not yet made manifest what we shall be. We know that, if he shall be manifested, we shall be like him; for we shall see him even as he is.'

In two of these passages the perfection set before us as our destiny is expressed in terms of likeness to our Lord Himself, the first of them being, of course, the scriptural warrant for the triumphant conclusion, already quoted, of Charles Wesley's 'Love Divine'. Such promises seem staggering to us, accustomed as we are to reducing the Gospel to more manageable proportions, but there they are, and they have haunted mankind ever since. This is what the Christian religion is about, or it is about nothing at all.

CHAPTER V

A DOCTRINE FOR TODAY

IF the contention of the preceding chapters is sound, there would appear to be special reasons, amounting almost to urgency, why attention should be drawn to it at the present time, when the truth it contains is being almost entirely neglected, and indeed in many quarters denied.

The scholar who has exercised the greatest influence on Christian thought in the last thirty years is Dr Karl Barth, and the movements which directly or indirectly derive their impetus from his writings tend to stress the divine otherness and man's utter inability to achieve anything himself. Similarly, Dr Rheinhold Niebuhr stresses continually man's persistent sinfulness. Many readers will be familiar with Dr John Baillie's *Invitation to Pilgrimage* in which he devotes one of his most interesting chapters to this topic. The issue is clearly stated in a quotation Dr Baillie cites from Professor Niebuhr's work. 'The question is whether the grace of Christ is primarily a power of righteousness which so heals the sinful heart that henceforth it is able to fulfil the law of love; or whether it is primarily the assurance of divine mercy for a persistent sinfulness which man never overcomes completely.' Dr Niebuhr declares firmly for the second alternative and has placed us all in his debt by his massive exposition of the assurance we have in Jesus Christ and of the measureless mercy of God, but the very cogency and brilliance of his contribution lay on us a corresponding responsibility to maintain our witness to the complementary truth. That the mercy of God is inexhaustible and available again and again for the persistent sinner is indeed an infinitely precious and an indispensable truth of the Gospel, but does it exhaust its meaning? Dr Niebuhr speaks of the Sermon on the Mount as an impossible ideal, yet holds it to be relevant. But if it is impossible, must it not in the end be regarded as little more than a rhetorical flourish? And is it in harmony with the character of our Lord and what we know of His dealings with men that He should so teach?

Dr Baillie himself compares this divergency of outlook with that which existed between St Paul and St James concerning faith and works. Both apostles were seized of an important truth and, although those truths were made to appear contradictory, in fact they were complementary. So in this matter we may well agree with Dr Niebuhr concerning not only the fact but the need for the continuous mercy of God. All of us who write or preach about the Doctrine of Christian Perfection must assuredly do this as our only defence against those who can and do so easily pour scorn on the great gulf between what we preach and what we practise. It may well be that the reluctance to preach the full gospel of the enabling, as well as the forgiving, grace of God springs from an unwillingness on our part to expose ourselves to such taunts; for most of us are vulnerable indeed, and the world in which we preach has come to regard pretension to sanctity as one of the most offensive and least tolerable sins. Sometimes this attitude takes the form of an inverted Pharisaism. Instead of pretending to be better than they are, men will go to great lengths to disclaim any moral worth, the one unforgivable thing in their view being to pose as better than they really are. By this means, they seek to evade the moral challenges of life. In the same way, a curious cult seems to have grown up whereby rich men pretend to be poor, a stupid perversion of the custom, which so long prevailed, of parading such wealth as one possessed and at any rate appearing rich if at all possible, even if one were not.

Wesley himself, as already noted, never claimed to have attained perfection, but he never shrank from proclaiming it as an essential part of the salvation Jesus brings, and similarly we dare not limit the potential scope and range of the Gospel. The vital content of the doctrine is surely that no limit whatever can be set to what God can accomplish in and through the believer. We cannot say, 'So far and no farther'. The only goal for every man is 'Perfection's sacred height'. In appreciating this fact it is important to avoid being led away into speculative theories as to whether in fact Christian perfection is permanently or even momentarily possible for any particular individual in this life. It is even less profitable to allow our minds to range over the men and women of our acquaintance and consider whether any of them qualify for such a description. We need to remind ourselves that men as we know them are not finished products. They are in process of becoming. Nor for Christians can the horizon be bounded by this life which is an anticipation of the fuller life to come:

> *Yet onward I haste*
> *To the heavenly feast:*
> *That, that is the fullness; but this is the taste.*

If we fail to recognize these truths, we shall be in danger of setting up some theoretical absolute standard of perfection, a kind of sum total of all the excellences, to which we expect all men immediately to conform, or be judged as failures accordingly. But to interpret perfection in this fashion is to ignore the whole method of God's gracious dealings with the human soul and to substitute a state of anxious frustration and a paralysing sense of inadequacy for that sense of perfect freedom which accompanies the joyful and spontaneous response of the believer to the promptings of the Holy Spirit. Perfection at any one moment consists not in conformity to some absolute rule but in the completeness of the response made at that moment to the love of God at whatever stage we may have arrived in our pilgrimage. Likeness to God is to be both the test of conduct on the journey and the goal that awaits us at the end of it.

This, however, in spite of what so many present-day theologians assert, is not humanism. For, as we have seen, sanctification, like justification, is a gift of God, not a human achievement. It can neither be bought with any price we can pay nor be achieved by any effort of which we are capable. We can neither earn nor deserve it. But God is waiting to bestow it upon us freely. To deny this possibility is not to be realist about the sinfulness of human nature but to disbelieve in the power of God to remake human nature. Indeed we may well ask what lower standard could ever be accepted by God or by man made in God's image. If we abandon perfection, what shall we retain? What, indeed, is worth retaining?

Furthermore, properly understood, belief in the doctrine of Christian perfection removes once for all the deadly snare of complacency. The loftiest external standard, such as the righteousness of the Scribes and Pharisees, is to be preferred to the limitless standard of Christian perfection if we desire to be self-satisfied. Men are complacent if they have too low an opinion of themselves and attain the standard they have set, not if they have seen the glory of God in Jesus Christ and heard His call.

Nor is the doctrine of Christian Perfection invalidated by the importance attached, especially by Continental theologians, to the eschatological element in the Gospel, that is, to the concern of the Gospel with the last things or the end of the world. Those who were present at or who have read about the Second Assembly of the World Council of Churches at Evanston will be aware that the main theme, 'Christ the Hope of the World', was very largely interpreted in terms of eschatology. The attainment of Christian Perfection by individuals or indeed by society under the transforming influence of the Holy Spirit played no part in the scheme of things. Such a theme is entirely foreign to the current trends of ecumenical theology. Now no one with even a casual knowledge of the New Testament would deny the large place occupied by the Christian hope and the Christian teaching about the last things. It is surely common ground among all Christians that the meaning of life is to be understood in dramatic terms. This is part of the heritage we have received from the Hebrews. God has a plan and purpose which is being worked out in history. As there was a beginning at creation, so there will be an end of the present process; time will be no longer but will be swallowed up in eternity. Nor can there be much doubt that our earliest fathers in the faith believed that the end of the present age was rapidly approaching. Scholars differ as to how far our Lord shared that view, but quite probably He did so to a considerable extent. The eminent scholars who emphasize this aspect of the Gospel have much to teach us and indeed the hopes connected with it are a permanent element in our understanding of the Gospel.

But the fact remains that nineteen hundred years have elapsed and the end is not yet. Nor is there any necessary reason to suppose it is likely to occur in this generation any more than in those which have preceded it. It is true, of course, that men have at last obtained the power to destroy civilization, and it may be that such a judgement may be visited on us unless men and nations turn from the wickedness of war to the paths of peace, but it seems doubtful whether even then the consequence would be complete extinction. However that may be, the nearness or otherwise of the end of this present age in no way affects the cardinal importance of the doctrine of Christian Perfection. Those who hold that our Lord's ethical teaching was simply intended as a temporary code applicable only to the brief period which it was expected would precede the end of the present age overlook the vital fact that our Lord's warrant for His teaching had nothing to do with the length of time this world would last, but was based on the character of God. We are to behave as sons of the Father, and we are to be perfect because our Father in heaven is perfect. God is Lord of time and space. He is the ever-living who was and is and is to come, and whether it be in this world which He has made, or in what for want of a better term we call eternity, His nature and His will are changeless. If the Church has a message of hope for bewildered and despairing men and women, such a message may, indeed must, be in the framework which includes the idea of a goal to which they and the whole creation are moving. But it must also speak to their present condition and bring them the power and help they so sorely need. This is an age when man has lost faith not only in God but also in man. This is true not only on the individual level but equally on the social and international level. Men are aware not only of the triumphs of modern science and the boundless resources made available to mankind, but also of man's moral failure to avail himself of these resources in a way that shall bring blessing to mankind. In this plight he needs to be reminded of God's mercy and forgiveness. But forgiveness is not enough. If it can be said without being misunderstood, men are bored with being forgiven. They do not doubt God's mercy; His willingness to forgive is accepted as part of His acknowledged character. But what they have no inkling of is that God is both able and willing to do something about them and about the world which seems to them to be drifting into irretrievable disaster. If we can convince them that neither they nor the world have slipped from the grasp of God beyond His power to help, we shall find them eager and ready to respond. In this connexion I recall a visit to a factory canteen on a commando campaign. At the conclusion of my brief address, when questions were invited, a man who had been playing patience and was apparently oblivious to what was going on suddenly looked up and the following dialogue ensued:

'Look, mister, you say that the world is in a mess because of man's sin?'

'Yes.'

'And you say that God is merciful and will forgive us our sins?'

'Yes.'

'What next, mister?'

'Well, isn't that enough to be going on with?'

'No, it isn't, because what's going to happen then? Are we going on sinning while the world gets worse and worse, till the whole thing blows up? Can't your God do better than that?'

How right my questioner was. Forgiveness is not enough. Heaven knows we all need forgiveness, but we need also to be made aware of the reality of God's power not only to forgive but also to remake humanity.

If the world is to move forward to a new and better age which shall witness fresh triumphs of the human spirit, help must come from the outside. Within himself man with all his knowledge and ingenuity has not the resources to enable him to use his new powers aright and extricate himself from his desperate plight.

But help has come from the outside. Jesus Christ has shown us in His life and death God's eternal purpose of holy love. He has shown us, too, what man is in

God's plan and purpose, and has made available for us through His Spirit the resources of divine grace whereby that purpose may be gloriously fulfilled now and in eternity.

If the foregoing is true, it means nothing less than that Methodism has a contribution to make to the thinking of the world Church of Jesus Christ today without which the message of that Church will be incomplete. It is a contribution which no other tradition is making or is likely to make. That is a daring claim, but it is supported by the facts. This is an aspect of the Gospel which the Holy Spirit appears to have entrusted to the people called Methodists to proclaim and to safeguard. During the two centuries of our separate existence it has been the dynamic of our evangelical activity. But we hold it in trust for the whole Church of God. Now it is ours to offer, as in return there is so much else that is ours to receive.

But first we need to be sure of it ourselves. The object of this book is to invite Methodists to examine their heritage afresh, and consider whether our tradition does not provide us with the supreme word to match this hour. The alternative is that our distinctive teaching has been a mistake. If that were so, it would seem that the world-wide Communion which has grown up in the course of two centuries as a result of missionary zeal has all the time been based on a foundation of error. 'Love Divine' must be scrapped, and with it all that is distinctive in our hymn-book and our discipline. There will remain only our organization, one of the most efficient instruments in Christendom, to be handed over to some other tradition with as little delay and disturbance as possible.

This alternative, however, needs only to be mentioned to be rejected. It is unthinkable so to dishonour our past. Rather let us look afresh at the rock whence we were hewn but repent that we have allowed ourselves to come perilously near to neglecting such a heritage. Let us pray that, under the guidance of the Holy Spirit, we may be enabled to play our distinctive part, in company with the whole Church of God, in proclaiming the Gospel to a perishing world.

Part II. A Doctrinal Examination

CHAPTER VI

GOD

'METHODISM takes the old theology of the Christian Church, but it takes one element which no other Christian Church has dared to put forward as a prominent feature of theology. In ours it is the very point from which we view all theology.'

So President John McClintock, of Drew University, described the place which Christian perfection, or, as he put it, the holiness of the human soul, heart, mind, and will, occupies in the Methodist understanding of the faith. 'It is the very point from which we view all theology.' If that be true, and such has been the whole contention of this book so far, there is a need for Methodist theologians to set forth the implications of the doctrine of Christian perfection for that whole range of doctrines enshrined in the historic creeds which form part of our common Christian heritage. This need is especially urgent at this time when the Churches, with their differing traditions, are drawing together to pool their theological and spiritual resources, in order that in co-operation if not yet in unity they may minister to the needs of mankind. The doctrine of Christian perfection is for us in our tradition a vantage ground from which we survey the whole field of Christian truth, and there would seem to be few, if any, of our cherished beliefs which do not shine with some new light when viewed from this standpoint.

The task outlined above will, I hope, engage the attention of our foremost Methodist theologians on both sides of the Atlantic. It consists of nothing less than the thinking out and expressing in formal terms of a systematic theology from this particular angle. All that can be attempted in the succeeding chapters is to review some of the central truths of our faith and suggest aspects of them which our Methodist emphases throw into greater relief. If by this means the point of view expressed in the earlier part of this volume is illustrated and in some degree sustained, others, whose training and equipment make them competent to do so, will doubtless address themselves to the task. I can think of no more valuable way in which our Church can make its contribution to the world Church of Jesus Christ.

Let us make a beginning by considering our belief in God. This is the most natural and appropriate place to begin, for two reasons: first, because what we believe about God determines what we believe about ourselves and about other people and ultimately about everything else, and secondly because, as we have already seen, the character of God is both the warrant for and the standard of all Christian behaviour. We are to be perfect because our Father in heaven is perfect and our actions are to be such as might be expected from sons of the Father.

The idea of Perfection is inseparable from the idea of God. When men have believed in many deities, each with limited authority, they have not necessarily attributed perfection to any of them, but wherever the idea has prevailed that God is One, by that very fact He has been thought of as perfect. If there is indeed a Being other and greater than ourselves who made us, other and greater than the universe who made that, by definition all the excellences meet in Him. He is, as it were, Himself the norm of perfection. Yet this kind of perfection is something radically different from that Christian perfection with which we are here concerned. We should not think lightly of the insights into God's nature granted to men outside the Christian revelation. These insights received their profoundest expression in the Old Testament. The opening verse of the nineteenth Psalm, 'The heavens declare the glory of God; and the firmament sheweth His handywork', sums up the experience of countless men in every age and land who have been moved to worship by the revelation of God's majesty and power in creation. That this is a true pathway to understanding something about God and His ways is vouched for by none other than Jesus Himself, whose teaching is studded with flowers and trees and birds and fields of golden corn.

Then, too, we can never ignore 'the light which lighteth every man coming into the world'. We think, for example, of the overwhelming sense of awe felt by Moses beside the burning bush, or by Isaiah in the temple, as they glimpsed something of the holiness of God. We recognize in the Hebrew prophets men who so responded to God's approach that they became the messengers of His truth to their day and generation. But when all these things have been taken into account, it is salutary to ask ourselves what sort of a Being we should conceive God to be if we depended solely upon them for our knowledge of God.

Nature, wonderful as it is, speaks with an uncertain voice and is but a broken fragment of the revelation of God. Nature is sometimes kind but sometimes cruel, and we must beware of making a selection from its evidence to suit our preconceived ideas. What of the hawk swooping on its prey or the moth drawn by light to its own destruction? It is sometimes said that God made the country but man made the town. It would be difficult to conceive a more misleading comparison. If we think of the Highlands of Scotland, we must think too of the swamps of Africa. And if men are responsible for the ugliness of the slums, there are places, too, which once were desert but now blossom as the rose.

Nor can it be claimed that the scientific interpretation of the universe, with which we are familiar, has altogether helped. For the Psalmist the earth was the centre of everything and the universe revolved round it; we know that in relation to the vastness of the universe our earth is but the tiniest speck. In the time of the Psalmist, and indeed until comparatively recently, it was believed that the universe had been created by a Being who within measurable time had said, 'Let there be light', and there was light; we now know that there has been life on the earth for a million years and that the world itself is older still. It is true that many scientists and others find every fresh discovery a source of wonder, revealing always a reality grander than had hitherto been imagined and redounding to the greater glory of God, but that is because they interpret these things in the light of a religious faith and experience drawn from other sources. For other scientists and a great host of ordinary men and women, the very uniformity of nature seems impersonal and suggests a universe which, however it started, now operates by mechanical processes.

At its best, the revelation of God in creation leaves unanswered all the most important questions we have to face. What sort of people ought we to be? On what principles should we make our choices? How should we meet temptation or endure sorrow? How should we live together? What kind of a society should we strive to establish? To these and similar questions natural religion affords no answer.

When we come to the revelation through great and good men and women, we are on surer ground. Many insights regarding God's character and will have come to men in this way. Ideals of righteousness, justice, and purity have been glimpsed and in varying degrees expressed. The source of these, we should gladly recognize, is none other than the living God Himself, who ever addresses the men and women He has made, seeking an entrance into their minds and hearts, and winning a response. In this connexion we think especially of the Hebrew prophets—of Amos thundering his denunciation of the social iniquities of his day, of Hosea, the prophet of God's mercy towards His unfaithful people, and supremely of the second Isaiah, whose prophecy of the suffering Servant was regarded, as many think, by our Lord Himself as affording a clue to the mystery of His own sufferings, and has certainly been so regarded by Christians ever since.

There is nothing surprising about this, for it was in the fullness of time that God sent His Son, and that full revelation is to be understood in the light of what had gone before.

But when all has been said that can be said along these lines, and full acknowledgement made of these and other ways whereby God has made Himself known to men, the fact remains that the gulf between what we know about God through Jesus and what we should have known in every other way had He not come is immeasurable.

Nineteen hundred years ago the eternal God, who was and is and is to be, became Man. 'The word became flesh and dwelt among us.' Or, as Charles Wesley expressed it in memorable verse:

> *Our God contracted to a span,*
> *Incomprehensibly made man.*

Christianity is an historical religion. It came into existence because at a particular time and place certain events happened. If they had not happened, there would have been no Christianity. Those events are set forth in the New Testament story. On the merely human level it is the most wonderful story in the world; but the central fact, we believe, is that it is a story about God, telling us what God did. It describes how God, by that act of self-disclosure, revealed Himself to be what otherwise in our wildest flights of imagination we should never have guessed Him to be. The story is not just an episode; it embodies eternal truth. As Jesus was in time, so God always has been and always will be. Primarily the Gospel is good news about God. On that truth the whole Christian religion rests; it is what makes Christianity Christianity and not some other religion.

The uniqueness of this revelation lies in what Jesus showed us of God's character and purpose. Since Jesus lived and taught, we know as we should never otherwise have known that God is Love. He is still Goodness and Power and Beauty, but in character and purpose He is Love. Indeed it is significant that this central attribute of Love colours for the Christian all the other attributes. A man, for example, brought up in the Christian tradition, who chooses to visit the countryside in preference to his church on a lovely Sunday morning and professes that he finds it easier to worship God that way, almost certainly invests the character of the God with whom he claims to have communion with qualities no contemplation of the beauty of nature would reveal, but only God in that revelation of Himself in Jesus Christ.

Furthermore, power in the sense of abstract force is meaningless. Its exercise is determined by the character of its possessor and in fulfilment of his purpose. Hence, belief in the Power of God becomes for the Christian belief in the power of Love. Paul himself recognized this when he wrote of 'Christ, the Power of God'.

The Way of Life set forth by Jesus as He taught the crowds on the Galilean hillside was exemplified by Him as He gave Himself utterly for us men and our salvation on that other hill without the city wall. Others may have said, 'Love one another'. He alone can say, 'Love one another, even as I have loved you'.

The tragedy of nineteen hundred years of Christian history is that men have refused to take His teaching seriously. When we find it running contrary to our own desires or to some supposed interest of our nation or community, we have sought to explain that our Lord did not really mean what He said. Or else, unable to expose any fallacy in it, we have had recourse to the unworthy subterfuge of elevating it out of sight as impracticable, too lofty for this workaday world. Do we realize that in so doing we both dishonour our Lord and debase the Gospel?

God made man in His own image and man's highest glory is to do God's works after Him. Every great achievement of the human spirit is a response to something in God. It is because man had seen the beauty of nature that he was led to work out his inspiration in abiding form and paint lovely landscapes and build beautiful cathedrals. It is because he had first listened to the song of the bird on the bough and the rustle of trees in the wind that he was led to find out musical tunes and devise instruments for their expression. As God's supreme blessing to men is His Love, expressed once for all in Jesus, so the supreme response of which we are capable is in the realm of character and conduct.

So understood, the principles of the Sermon on the Mount, otherwise impracticable and indeed even nonsensical, become not only reasonable but inevitable. 'If a man compel thee to go with him one mile, go with him twain.' Why should I? 'Love your enemies and pray for them that persecute you.' This goes beyond the most exacting requirements of human decency and uprightness. Yes, but that is precisely what Jesus did. We can only find fault with His teaching if we reject His character. And His character is the character of the eternal God.

It can hardly be claimed that the rejection of His claims and the reduction of His standards have been an unqualified success. What if after all it is we who are impractical? What if this world is really God's world and will therefore only work God's way? What if Christian Perfection is not impractical idealism but God's purpose for us and what He offers through Jesus Christ? It then becomes the only way of life for men and women made in God's image and redeemed by Jesus Christ. We are therefore to be perfect for the sole but compelling reason that God is perfect and we are His children.

CHAPTER VII

MAN

THE implications of the Doctrine of Christian Perfection on the Christian doctrine of man are almost too obvious to need stating. And yet there is no subject on which there is more doubt and disagreement today than this, and no subject on which men are in greater need of the enlightenment which the Gospel brings. For one thing, it is a subject which forces its attention upon the most casual and careless of men.

Many people seem to be able to go through life for the most part without thinking very much about God. They may dismiss the subject as one on which they are unable to form any opinion, or even if they have views about Him they may relegate them to the back of their minds as not of immediate and urgent importance; but they cannot do that with man. An absentee God is quitea common idea, but there can be no absentee man. Our lives are bound up at every point with those of other men. Their presence calls for perpetual adjustment on our part. There are men and women in our own families living under the same roof; there are men we meet every day at work or every week in sport. There are remote men we read about who make the laws under which we live, and men remoter still who manufacture ballistic missiles which one day may fall on us. Even the least reflective among us must sometimes ask: 'What is man?'

And what answer will he receive? It depends on whom he asks. Many answers could be given, each of which contains part of the truth. Physically, man is a highly intricate piece of mechanism which has evolved in the

long course of the ages; more is known about man's origin
in that sense than ever before. More significant are man's
mental processes, and in our own day these have been the
subject of much study and research in the new field of
psychology. Interesting, however, as all this may be, it
only helps us to answer the secondary questions about
man. Not that those questions are unimportant. Knowledge of man's physical make-up, of how his body works,
is essential for his well-being. In this life on earth man
must needs express himself through his body, and the
fitter that body can be, the greater the freedom a man will
have and the wider the scope and range of his activities.
Of much greater moment is the understanding of man's
mind, for it is at this point that we are made aware of a
faculty in man which natural religion overlooks and which
the materialistic interpretation of the universe ignores—
the supremacy of mind. We may go back as far as we can
trace, but the human mind can still ask what was before
that. We may go out to the very edge of space, but the
human mind will ask what is beyond that. If at first man
may seem insignificant in comparison with the vastness
of the universe, the positions are reversed when it is
realized that man can make the comparison but the
universe cannot.

In spite of all this, however, these matters fall short of
the really vital question concerning man. They deal
with how his body functions and how his mind works.
But what we really need to know, apart from which
everything else we know will only prove tantalizing and
frustrating, is why there is such a creature as man at all.
What purpose lies behind the creation and development
of mankind? In the light of the supremacy of mind we
have already noted, it would seem that the whole created
world provides the stage for the unfolding drama of the
human story. What does it mean? How should it end?
In the light of this, how should we behave? How should

we use the powers we now possess? At this point there is nothing but confusion in the minds of men. Man who has solved so many problems seems baffled by the problem of himself. Having wrested so many secrets of the universe that have lain hidden from the foundation of the world, he remains himself the unsolved enigma. He may know more than ever before about his origin but there is little satisfaction in that if he knows less about his destiny. While that remains true, can we reasonably expect anything other than chaos and conflict in human affairs? How can men hope to live together happily unless there is some agreement about the true nature and destiny of man and the purpose of human life? This state of affairs is reflected all too accurately in the disappearance of standards of behaviour accepted by all. There is widespread confusion about the very basis of right and wrong, and the characteristic question of the age is 'Why should I?' In many countries violence and the rule of force are quite unashamedly employed if they serve political ends, and in our own land breaches not only of the law but of ordinary decent codes of behaviour are increasing in number and causing alarm among all who are concerned with these things. It is difficult to conceive of any greater boon that could come to man at the present juncture when his future hangs in the balance and may issue either in hitherto undreamed of achievement and happiness or unparalleled misery, perhaps extinction itself, than that this uncertainty about man's true nature and destiny should give way to such a generally accepted recognition of his status as would effectively re-establish right moral standards in private and public relationships.

Man has lost faith in his brother man. Speaking generally, we only trust one another as far as we can see; indeed such an attitude is openly encouraged by notices for our protection in public places. Humanity is corrupt and in danger of going bad before our very eyes. But the worst is that we have ceased to expect it to be anything else. Just as the financial structure depends for its stability on 'credit', lack of which results in collapse, so somehow faith in man must be restored or the whole fabric of social life will disintegrate in irretrievable ruin.

It is precisely at this point that the doctrine of Christian Perfection speaks the reassuring and transforming word, by telling us that the truth about man is that he is made by God and for God. In the intention of his Maker, man is destined to be perfect. This may seem to be flying in the face of the facts as we know them, and we shall need to consider these facts at a later stage. Meanwhile, let us recognize that the truth about any of us is not to be discerned in how we appear to our friends or our enemies or even to ourselves at the moment. No one of us is a finished product. We are all in process of becoming and can only be properly defined in terms of the intention and purpose of God who made us. If, as we have seen, the first and central fact about the story which gave rise to our Christian faith is that it is a story about God, bringing the good news of His character and purpose of love, the second fact is that it is a story about man, bringing good news of him. Our Lord Jesus was very God and very Man, which does not mean partly God and partly Man, but wholly God and wholly Man. It has been a different thing to live this life of ours since Jesus lived it. Just as surely as He alone has revealed to us the character and purpose of the eternal God, so He has revealed, as none other, man's true nature and destiny. He has shown men what they are and what they may become.

Of all the mistaken ideals that have led men astray in recent times, none has been more disastrous than that of independence. Its danger lies largely in the fact that its achievement requires qualities which are in themselves admirable, such as courage, perseverance, and self-respect. Who has not felt the manly appeal of Longfellow's

'Village Blacksmith' who 'owed not any man'? In the political and international realm, self-determination is an ideal which has won widespread recognition in the democratic world and is accepted almost automatically as a desirable thing. But the Kingdom of Heaven is not a democracy. Though independence is no doubt greatly to be preferred to vassalage or slavery, the nations must learn that interdependence is essential if civilization is to survive, and in individual and personal life independence is an utterly false and indeed impossible aim. We cannot be independent of our fellow man; the richest man in the world depends on other people, first to recognize the validity of his wealth, whatever form it takes, and then to render him countless services in exchange for it. And to talk of being independent of God is lunatic, indeed blasphemous; the truth is that we are all utterly dependent on Him, and that is not our shame but our glory. On what does the supposedly independent man base his independence, and how does he maintain it? If he claims to stand on his own feet, how did he get them? Whence came that strong right arm and those endowments of mind and heart in which he puts his trust? And how long will all these powers endure? To ask these questions is to reveal the absurdity of it all. There is only one firm foundation for any man's present well-being and future hope, namely that he is the object of God's unceasing love and care. Nay more, that he is somebody for whom Christ died and rose again. And He died to make us not comfortable nor even happy but good, yea perfect, which means that ultimately the Christian view of man must be optimistic. To be optimistic about human nature is regarded in many quarters as a hallmark of shallowness and superficiality. It is held to involve an inadequate appreciation of the terrible facts of sin and the judgement which follows it. The only realistic view of human nature, we are told, is pessimistic. Well, we must indeed be pessimistic. We can hardly avoid it if we open a news-paper or switch on the radio. Children of God, did the New Testament writer say? Of course, and that is why we are pessimists. If we were not children of God, the things we plan and sometimes carry out would not be so ghastly. It is that children of God should behave like this that makes it so awful. But by the same token the pessimism, if it is the right sort of pessimism, is the obverse of a deeper and more abiding optimism. For that is the Gospel. It is good news about God and good news about man.

It is this which separates man from the rest of creation. Man has much in common with other created beings and things, but he is unique in that he alone is not only created by God but addressed by Him. God made mountains and stars and the beasts of the field, but He does not address them. Only man can know that God made him. Only man can respond to God, or, if he chooses, withhold that response. Speaking generally, man is also intellectually superior to the rest of the animal creation, but, as Professor Jessop has pointed out in his book *Science and the Spiritual*, it is not in that field that man's uniqueness is to be found, but in his moral and spiritual capacity. Unlike all other created beings, man is capable of entertaining and pursuing ideals. He is aware of a category all his own, that of value. He can describe something as good, and something else as better. He can, and constantly does, criticize other people, and, what is more important, he can criticize himself. He, and he alone, is endowed with that remarkable faculty called Conscience. In the operation of conscience, as we are well aware, human factors play their part, so that conscience does not speak in an identical manner to men in different centuries or in different environments; but when every allowance is made for these contingent elements, the fact remains that the voice of conscience, however mixed up with these other things, is the voice of God. To sum this up and bring it into direct relation to our present theme, we may say that man alone can conceive the idea of perfection, whether it be perfect man or a perfect society. But their own possible perfection and any idea of a Utopia are alike outside the range of animals.

The message of the Gospel is that this moral and spiritual dimension which characterizes humanity derives from the fact that God Himself is perfect, and made man in His image, and in Jesus has revealed His eternal purpose of love which will never abandon us to our sin nor let us go until that purpose is achieved.

CHAPTER VIII

SIN

HOW sin entered into the world is an unsolved mystery and will probably remain so. Certainly it was no part of creation as willed by God. Indeed by definition it is the wilful defiance by men of His will and purpose. But equally certainly God has permitted it, and it is difficult for us with our limited understanding to conceive how it could have been otherwise, for the perfection which God wills us to attain can have no significance for us apart from the possibility of its opposite. Similarly, we cannot entertain the idea of light apart from the idea of darkness, nor the idea of knowledge apart from the idea of ignorance. There is a perpetual conflict between light and darkness, knowledge and ignorance, good and evil. As light increases darkness grows less; as knowledge advances ignorance is banished, and the Christian believer holds the faith that ultimately good will overcome evil.

The complete response to God wherein perfection consists is no enforced obedience but a freely given allegiance to God who has given Himself to us in love. It appears that, knowing the risks involved in its possible misuse, God gave men the freedom to make this response and therefore the freedom to withhold it, for only so could His purpose of love be achieved and a true fellowship of men with God come into being. This needs to be borne in mind when we are tempted, as most of us are on occasion, to question the wisdom or the love of God in the light of the appalling consequences of man's sin. Without belittling in the slightest degree the dreadful nature of these consequences, we should be comforted by the reflection that God, who foresaw them, yet thought it better thus rather than that men should be deprived of that moral quality which is their distinctive characteristic.

Sin, then, for the purposes of this discussion, must be regarded as wilful disobedience of God. For the religious man that is always its essential content. Very often it also involves wrong behaviour towards other people. In this world where we are bound so closely to our fellow-men, and where, as we have seen, there is no holiness but social holiness, sin almost inevitably finds its expression in relation to other people, but its prime content is that it is disobedience of God. 'Against Thee, Thee only have I sinned and done that which is evil in Thy sight.' In the last analysis sin is human pride setting itself against God. Men choose their own ways in preference to His, and are motivated by self-interest rather than the fulfilment of His will.

In this sin we are all involved, which is what is meant by the familiar but often misunderstood expression 'original sin'. However sin entered into the world, its presence and its reality are evident everywhere. Not only are individuals all sinners but the human race as a whole is a fallen race. Every child who is born inherits the physical, mental, and spiritual characteristics of humanity. This does not imply that a new-born baby can be held responsible for sins committed by his immediate or his more remote ancestors. That would be a monstrous suggestion. But he takes his place, as it were, in the stream of humanity, and it is a tainted stream. He, therefore, inherits a tendency to self-interest, the roots of which lie deeper than we often care to acknowledge and go right back in human history. In this connexion Dr Harold Roberts in his book *Jesus and the Kingdom of God*, draws an illuminating contrast between original sin and original guilt. We all inherit the tendency which makes sin very probable, but it only becomes guilt when we yield to that tendency. Jesus differed from us, not in being free from that tendency, which would have meant that He was not really Man, but in that by never yielding to it He directed His energies at every point towards the doing of the perfect will of God. In that sense our Lord's perfection is different from that which ours can ever be, for our perfection will be the fruit of His redemptive grace.

As perfection involves communion with God, so the consequence of sin is separation from God, resulting in the corruption of a man's whole being. Once again, this estrangement from God finds expression in a thousand different ways, as we can observe in ourselves and in the world all round about us. It brings misery and unhappiness not only to the sinner but to the community to which he belongs. The Christian explanation of the state of the world today is that ultimately it derives from men's insistence on their own will instead of God's. This is in fact God's world where He reigns supreme. It will only really work His way. If men persist in preferring their own way it means that they are trying to live in an unreal world which simply does not exist. That can only lead to disaster.

This is judgement, which is both inevitable and real. It is 'the wrath of God revealed from heaven against all ungodliness and unrighteousness of men'. Its existence is terrible, but its absence would be even more so. 'It is a fearful thing to fall into the hands of the living God'; yes, but it would be more fearful not to do so. For the wrath of God, so terrible, is not different from the love of God. God cannot deny Himself: He is always love, not sometimes love and sometimes something else. His wrath is one expression of His love. If a man could persistently live for selfish ends in antagonism to God's will and no unpleasant consequences ensue, that would be disaster indeed. We deplore the frightful toll that war exacts in human wretchedness and misery, but the really deplorable thing is the vast moral failure of which war is the outward sign. If nations could hate one another and pursue selfish ends in defiance of all morality and still live together comfortably, that would be a worse state of affairs, for it would mean that God had abandoned us to our sin. 'Whom the Lord loveth, He chasteneth.' His purpose in His wrath is not vindictive, but redemptive. This is the gospel and it speaks to us of hope. Sin is the unspeakable thing it is because it is an intruder. God is far too loving to overlook or condone it. He visits us with His wrath because only so can He truly love us. That is why we do right to speak of the problem of evil. There is only a problem of evil because there is a problem of goodness. There is only original sin because there is also original goodness. If that were not so, evil would present no problem at all. While we are all painfully aware of the downward drag of sin, we must also be gratefully conscious of the upward pull of goodness. The very expression 'the Fall of Man' implies that there is an estate from which man fell, and the message of the gospel is that through the forgiving and transforming grace of God sinful man can be restored to goodness.

We do well to remind ourselves of the fact of goodness which persists in spite of all man's waywardness and folly. Dr George Macleod has described the Fall of Man as the story of Man, the Gardener, who defied co-operation with his Maker, but can never quite forget what the Garden once looked like. And indeed in the mercy of God none of us can finally rest content in our sin. Jesus did indeed speak of the possibility of the light in us becoming darkness, that is, of our spiritual vision becoming so distorted that we might even say, 'Evil, be thou my good'. But none of us would ever say of the worst man we knew that his plight was so hopeless. Rather do we feel about all men, including ourselves, that our hearts and minds are a miniature battlefield where on a small scale the age-long conflict between good and evil is being waged. When Paul penned the celebrated verse, 'The good which I would I do not but the evil which I would not that I practise', he was describing the experience of us all. In that very verse he suggests that the deepest and most permanent element in our make-up is that which, however unavailingly, desires the good.

Many evidences could be cited of this recognition on the part of men that goodness belongs and evil is an intruder to be resisted. I choose one from the field of the relatively new science of psychology. An otherwise normal and healthy boy entertained a quite irrational dislike of his father which was spoiling the life of the family. Under psychiatric treatment an incident of which the boy was not aware in his conscious self was brought to light and the trouble was dispelled. A normal enough occurrence, no doubt, but the significant thing is that the state of disharmony was recognized as unnatural and calling for treatment. No one thinks of taking boys to psychotherapists because they get on well with their fathers; that is how things should be between father and son, and indeed in all human relationships. Goodness is not news and does not hit the headlines. It is crime which is notable and merits special attention.

So man, in the purpose of his Creator, is essentially good, and our ultimate view of him must be optimistic. God made man in His own image, and through sin that image has been marred and defaced, often almost beyond recognition. But it has not been destroyed; otherwise, there would be no gospel to preach, for there would be nothing left in man to be appealed to. This is not to make light of sin and its dreadful consequences. The world is full of men and women who are perishing, and the plight of mankind is almost too terrible to contemplate. If man were left to his own resources, an attitude of unrelieved pessimism would be justified. But to avert such final ruin, God Himself became man and identified Himself in a redeeming way with our sin. Our sin was His shame, our suffering His sorrow, and our redemption the only satisfaction He sought.

He died that we might be forgiven,
He died to make us good.

CHAPTER IX

FORGIVENESS

IT is often remarked that modern man has no sense of sin, and we have already noted the absence of any widespread sense of moral need. The preacher's greatest obstacle is not to persuade men that God will forgive them but to persuade them that they need His forgiveness. Such a state of affairs, however, seems to me to require further examination, especially as it runs counter to what has already been said concerning man's uniqueness in this respect. If it were established that in absolute fact man, as we know him today, has developed into a being in whom the sense of sin is entirely absent, it would follow that he has become deficient in the one distinctive characteristic which marks him out from the rest of creation. I do not believe, however, that anything of the sort has occurred. When we speak of modern man having no sense of sin, we merely mean that many, though by no means all, of our fellow-men appear, as far as we can observe, to live their lives day by day without being oppressed by an acute consciousness of personal guilt which robs them of all peace of mind and will continue to do so until it is removed. That I believe to be true and a good deal can be said by way of explanation.

To begin with, the description just given is relatively superficial. That is to say, that while it may accurately describe the top of our minds, it might be very wide of the mark if we were considering the bottom of our hearts. We know, for example, what a large part the psychologists tell us the sense of guilt plays in all sorts of nervous troubles which on the surface betray no sign that they are so caused.

Furthermore, the man who would insist most strenuously that he had no sense of sin himself is often very much aware of other people's sins, and thereby makes nonsense of his own avowal, unless indeed he professes to be the one sinless being in a world of sinners. And all of us, however insensitive we may appear to be to our own moral failures, are to a greater or less degree appalled by the collective failure of mankind. Indeed it may be urged that the desperate state of humanity, at the very time when man's mastery of the powers of the universe would otherwise afford him the prospect of hitherto undreamed of happiness and glory, so tends to colour all our thought as to relegate to the background our own individual moral need. In a vague kind of way and with varying degrees of intensity, we recognize that ultimately the problem of society is the problem of the units of which it is composed, but the natural attitude of most of us is that we are neither personally responsible for the plight of mankind nor able to do anything about it. 'In a perfect world', we say, 'these things wouldn't happen, but the world is not perfect, nor the men and women in it.' Most of us would be honest enough to include ourselves in this description, but with a feeling of philosophical resignation about it, rather than a confession of guilt and shame. 'We must face facts. None of us is as good as we ought to be, but that's the way the world is made.'

If this is at all a fair account of the way most men react to the contemporary situation, it only needs a little reflection to see that what is really lacking is not so much a sense of sin as any idea of perfection. The easy-going and often fatalistic acceptance of men and women as not as good as they ought to be bears eloquent testimony to this. If the best that can be hoped for is that though men will go on sinning, God's mercy is broader and deeper than their sin, that attitude has much to commend it. But if we ever begin to take Jesus seriously, and measure

ourselves by the standard of His teaching and His character, if we ever glimpse the vision of the Kingdom of God
on earth, such an attitude becomes intolerable and
blasphemous.

A recovery of the idea of Christian Perfection as no
impractical dream, but the purpose of God for men and
for the world would re-awaken in men that sense of moral
need which would make them willing and able to receive
the forgiveness of God, and that would be the first step
towards moral renewal. The Pharisee in the parable was
indeed by every recognized standard a better man than
the publican, but because he had no sense of need, his
prayer could not be heard. He was the victim of his own
complacency. But the publican, overcome by a realiza-
tion of his utter unworthiness, could receive the forgiving
grace of God.

Forgiveness, we have seen, is not enough, but it remains
our primary need; for as the consequence of sin is separation from God, the consequence of forgiveness is our
restoration to unity with God. Until that happens, God's
gracious purposes for us cannot even begin to be fulfilled.
We need to distinguish between the forgiveness of sin and
the removal of its material consequences. The penitent
thief was not brought down from the cross on which he
hung, but he was readmitted into fellowship. It was to
bring men back into fellowship with the Father that Jesus
came.

To accept His offer involves a restored relationship not
only to God, but also to other people. Nowhere is the
social nature of holiness, and indeed of salvation itself,
made more evident in the New Testament than in relation to forgiveness. Consider, for example, the significance of the teaching about forgiveness in the Lord's
Prayer, given to the disciples in response to their request,
'Lord, teach us to pray'. There is nothing casual or
fortuitous about the model our Lord set before them.

Note the repeated use of the plural pronoun—'Our Father', 'Give us this day'. First God is to be addressed as the Father of all men, and then He is to be given His rightful place—'Hallowed be Thy name'. Then follows the prayer which can only be sincerely uttered by those whose wills are in harmony with His and who make the doing of His will their dominant desire—'Thy Kingdom come, Thy will be done'. Then follows the simple and natural petition for the material gifts on which life itself depends; this is in a form which recognizes our dependence on God and each other—'Give us our daily bread'. So far this ideal prayer might be prayed by ideal people, but then comes the confession which by now must surely be trembling on the lips of all who are not hopelessly unaware of their spiritual need. For we have not lived as sons of the one Father, nor given Him His rightful place; the accomplishment of His will and the establishment of His Kingdom have not been our dominant desire; our lives have not been ordered in the light of our dependence on Him and on our fellows. So, logically and inevitably, comes the prayer for forgiveness; but note its form— 'Forgive us . . . as we forgive'. We are immediately reminded of the parable of the unmerciful servant who had to be taught that he could not receive God's forgiveness free but sell his own at a price. When Jesus said, 'If ye forgive men their trespasses, your heavenly Father will also forgive you. But if ye forgive not men their trespasses, neither will your Father forgive your trespasses', He was not laying down some arbitrary condition, but reminding us of the very nature of mankind. It is not as though God were insisting on some bargain without which He would withhold His forgiveness. It is that our re-admission to fellowship with God involves us in a family relationship with our fellow-men. Our sonship of God is not a private and individual affair but one we share with all His children. We are members of God's universal family, where we have our place as forgiven sinners, but where the disposition to forgive must also govern our relationship with others, for whom Jesus died as He died for us.

This same willingness to be forgiven and also to forgive is necessary for the well-being of mankind at every level. The inward disposition to forgive is the cement by which every human society is bound together. More homes are wrecked by unwillingness to forgive than by wrongdoing. Nothing so spoils the fellowship of a church as the harbouring of grudges and the remembrance of real or imagined slights. How these things poison the relationships of nations is patent to all. So with the family of God. The elder brother in the parable with his blameless record was excluded from the family joy by this very thing. Nobody else kept him outside. His father besought him to enter, and the door was open, but his own vindictive attitude had poisoned his nature and he could not bring himself to cross the threshold.

The acceptance of forgiveness, therefore, while primarily our response to God's offer through Jesus Christ, is bound up with our relationship with other people, and this remains true at every stage of our spiritual pilgrimage. Goodness involves right relationship with God and with our fellow-men. Salvation and holiness can only be understood in this twofold setting.

So far we have said nothing about what is usually called the Atonement. The meaning of that word is clear if we split it up into its component parts and think of it as the At-one-ment. We have already seen that the result of forgiveness is the restoration of the broken fellowship between God and man. But how does the death of Jesus accomplish this? What do we mean when we sing 'He died that we might be forgiven'? There have been many theories about this and it is, of course, entirely right that we should bring the best thought of which God has made us capable to bear on this all-important and fascinating theme. But while there may well be some truth in all the theories, I do not believe that the whole truth is in any of them. Fortunately the Church is committed to no particular theory but to the fact of the Atonement as a glorious experience open to all, however wise or however simple.

But here again it may be fairly claimed that the doctrine of Christian perfection makes a valuable contribution by helping us to bear constantly in mind that God's supreme concern throughout is with the kind of people we become. His purpose and intention is that we shall be perfect. This is a most necessary safeguard against all views of forgiveness which reduce it to a weak or sentimental thing. Men may 'forgive' one another out of an easy-going indifference. A human father may behave in that way to his son in the mistaken belief that he is being kind when in reality he is endangering his boy's whole moral character. God loves us too much to let us off in that way. But equally God is not concerned with the mechanical vindication of some abstract law which when violated demands that some price must be extorted before forgiveness can operate. Some of the theories of the Atonement propounded by theologians have attempted to define it in terms of an algebraic equation or a legal transaction; but we are dealing with Love, which scorns mathematics and has nothing in common with a court of law.

God's one aim is that we shall be perfect, and the first step towards that end is that we shall realize our need of forgiveness and accept it freely from Him. There are no other conditions. 'If we confess our sins, He is faithful and *just* to forgive us our sins.'

If, however, this great mystery will always baffle our efforts to explain it, we can at any rate observe its operation beyond all doubt in the redemptive death of our Lord and its effect in the hearts of men. One of the hardest lessons to learn about forgiveness between men is that, if it is to come about, the initiative rests not with the one who has done the wrong but with the one who has suffered it. At first sight this sounds unreasonable; surely the most that can be expected of a man who has received an injury is that he should nurse no resentment and be willing, if approached, to forgive and resume friendly relations. But how many breaches between men have never been healed for just that reason. The man who has committed the offence is often too ashamed to think that he could ever be re-admitted into the fellowship he feels he has forfeited by his conduct. Illogical as it may seem, if the relationship is to be restored, the onus is on the wronged person to make the first move and let it be known that he on his side is willing and indeed anxious for a reconciliation. So it is between God and man. Whatever else is obscure about the Atonement, this is crystal clear. Its origin is in the heart of God; it was His initiative. God broke through the barriers which man's sin had erected between himself and God; 'God was in Christ reconciling the world unto Himself'. How different and how much less significant it would have been if Paul had felt constrained to write: 'Christ was in the world reconciling God and man.'

But it was no benevolent invitation to an easy-going compromise that He issued. His demands were absolute, and He never abated them. He called men to repentance and to perfection. But as He never let men off, neither did He ever let them go, and so ensued the terrible but glorious story of His Passion. It is the most terrible story in the world because we see in it as nowhere else the appalling nature of sin. We live in a grey world. None of us is pure white and none of us is altogether black; we are different shades of grey. But when Jesus was crucified, black met white. To gaze on the Cross of Jesus and realize that those responsible for that ghastly crime were respectable men, leaders in Church and State, animated by the kind of motive that animates us, is to be done for ever with any casual or lighthearted view of sin. We see there as nowhere else what our sins do to God and how wide is the gulf which separates us from Him. But if we turn from that and fix our gaze on the central figure and hear Him say 'Father, forgive them . . .', we begin to realize how divine love deals with human sin, bridging the gulf so that we are separated no longer. For so it has proved in the experience of men. It began when the first disciples who had forsaken Him at Calvary were received back into His fellowship and commissioned to be His messengers; and it has continued through the centuries, so that whenever and wherever men have seen the love of God in Jesus Christ and allowed their own love to go out to Him in return, the power of sin has been broken, and they have been aware of a new and transforming power released within them which has brought moral and spiritual victory and abiding peace.

CHAPTER X

IMMORTALITY

I DO not intend to suggest by the title of this chapter that men are necessarily immortal by nature. That does not seem to be the teaching of the Bible, which is concerned rather with the new life which God gives them. Death is not the end. After death there is resurrection, and God's purpose is that His faithful servants shall continue in a new manner the life which He has given them. That life is an immortal life.

There is no part of our faith to which in its various aspects the doctrine of Christian Perfection is more relevant than to the Christian hope of immortality. Conversely, there is no part of our faith which has a greater bearing on the idea of perfection than this belief in immortality. These two truths belong to and illuminate each other. It would be quite untrue to say that one is the obverse of the other and therefore that they are as inseparable as, say, the two sides of a penny. Each could be held separately. It is possible to believe in Christian Perfection but disbelieve in immortality; many people, on the other hand, do believe in immortality who have no concept of Christian Perfection. But it may be claimed that for its full significance each of these two truths needs to be interpreted in the light of the other, and shrinks in significance, being much less worthwhile, without it. As we shall see, the hope of immortality in its highest expression concerns the quality of life hereafter rather than its endless prolongation, and God's offer of perfection and challenge to it is infinitely more thrilling if it is related not only to the brief period of our life on earth but to His eternal purpose for which this life is a preparation.

There appear to me to be urgent reasons why the

doctrine of immortality, comparatively neglected in our preaching in recent times, should be restored to its historic position as a fundamental doctrine of our faith. For such assuredly it was in the beginning. That indeed is how Christianity began.

It was our Lord's resurrection, His conquest of sin *and death*, which gave initial impetus to the Christian movement though three days before it had appeared to have received its death blow. It may well be that there are elements in our historic faith which could be dispensed with without the whole edifice collapsing, but belief in immortality is not one of them. Historically speaking it is the core of the message. The last article of the creed, 'and the life everlasting', is also the crown of the creed. The gift of God is eternal life. 'This is the promise which He promised us, even the life eternal.' Salvation is salvation here and now, but also in eternity. This is the splendid structure of the Christian faith. The Eternal entered into time, lived, died, and rose again, not in order that we might be reconciled to God for the remainder of the three score years and ten, but for ever. This is the Christian interpretation of history, which declares that all things will be summed up in Christ. Remove this belief, and the Christian faith becomes an entirely different and altogether less significant thing.

And yet it is not difficult to understand the fashion in recent years of relegating the preaching of the Christian hope to the background. Several reasons have combined to bring this about. To begin with, belief in immortality is a matter of faith. It may rightly be said that that applies to every article of the creed, but it applies to this one in a special way. Most of the other articles are concerned with the interpretation of certain acknowledged facts, such as the existence of the created world or the events concerning our Lord's life and death, but when we come to consider immortality, what is involved is whether there is a world

at all other than this world we now inhabit. The rationalists maintain that there is not, or at any rate that if
there is *we* shall never see it. In their view it is impossible
for human personality to survive the shock of physical
death. The mind, they say, is a product of the brain
and when the brain ceases all mental faculties cease, too.
What we call the soul is not only physical in origin, it is
an inseparable part of the physical organism, so that
bodily existence is essential for its life. Man is just a highly
intricate and complicated machine; when the machine
stops, that is the end of him.

Now there is no proof that this is not so, unless we accept
the evidence of the spiritualists, to which we will turn later;
but what we must always remember is that there is no
proof that it is so. To hold the rationalist point of view is as
much a matter of faith as to hold the Christian belief in
immortality. Reason does not prove the rationalist's case,
nor, as I think, does it make it probable. The name 'rationalist' in this sense seems to be a misnomer; I would rather
describe those who hold this view as 'materialists'.

Against this, the Christian view is that our belief in
immortality, while not indeed susceptible of proof, is
much more reasonable. After all, it is not only concerning
what happens after death, but also in relation to most
things in life that 'we walk by faith, not by sight'; a child,
for example, can never anticipate the experience of being
grown up. Not only is the next world hidden from us,
but so also is next week and what it holds in store. This
condition, under which we perforce live, of constantly
advancing into a future all unknown may at times be
very tantalizing, but he would be an unusually brave,
not to say foolhardy man who, if afforded the opportunity,
would venture to lift the veil which hides the future from
us. Most of us would acknowledge that it is in God's
gracious providence that things are ordered thus, and
that the faith required of us is such as to produce a quality

of character which could be acquired in no other way. If that is true about our future in this world, how much more applicable to the world that is to come.

We can surely believe the same providence to be at work in preparing for us a life hereafter, because there would seem to be something which is, and which is meant to be, permanently unsatisfying about this present life. So Adelaide Anne Procter rightly makes this a subject for thanksgiving.

> *I thank Thee, Lord, that Thou hast kept*
> > *The best in store:*
> *We have enough, yet not too much*
> > *To long for more—*

and again

> *I thank Thee, Lord, that here our souls,*
> > *Though amply blest,*
> *Can never find, although they seek,*
> > *A perfect rest.*

We are pilgrims on a journey. This life is no aimless wandering, we have a goal to reach; but we have not yet arrived. So it is written of the Hebrew heroes of old. 'These all died in faith, not having received the promises, but having seen them and greeted them from afar and having confessed that they were strangers and pilgrims on the earth.'

A second reason for our failure to preach the Christian hope is the suggestion that there is something unworthy, not only in dwelling on the details of the bliss hereafter, but even in the desire itself for immortality. Dr Julian Huxley has described this as man's rationalization of selfish desires. But this is to beg the whole question. If the rationalists are right in their materialistic interpretation, some such explanation must be sought. But what if they are not right? In any event, if a man takes life at all seriously, how can he help thinking about this question? Death is one of the governing facts of life. It is one of the

few things we can be certain about in this uncertain world;
all human life inevitably comes to an end. Is it suggested
that we should behave like ostriches and ignore the whole
matter? What if God has set eternity in the human
heart? What if He has planned that we should so live
here as to be fitted for a fuller and ampler life? If He has,
it is as natural and proper that we should entertain such
thoughts and ponder their significance as it is that we
should be hungry for food and take steps to satisfy the
hunger. Furthermore, it should not be assumed that it is
only our own immortality about which we are concerned. What about our loved ones? Their life is as brief
and uncertain as our own and there is surely nothing
selfish in thinking about them.

There appears to me to be a real danger of falling into
a kind of false spirituality in this connexion. I am never
entirely happy with St Francis Xavier's well-known
hymn

> *My God, I love Thee—not because*
> *I hope for heaven thereby,*
> *Nor yet because who love Thee not*
> *Are lost eternally.*

St Francis Xavier was a missionary saint of outstanding
devotion and that may very well have been his own
attitude, though I understand that the translation of the
hymn fails to do justice to the original, and recent writers
even question whether St Francis was the author; but I
find it difficult to invite a congregation to join in professing
such disinterestedness.

> *Not with the hope of gaining aught:*
> *Not seeking a reward.*

Surely the realism of our Lord's teaching is to be preferred
where the idea of reward and punishment is unequivocally
present: 'Great is your reward in heaven.'

The third factor which has contributed to the neglect

of the theme of immortality in current preaching is the natural and healthy reaction against the kind of other-worldliness which led men so to concentrate on the thought of the next world as to make themselves unfit to live in this one. We can all recall hymns which, if taken seriously, could only lead to the conclusion that life in this present world is a regrettable necessity to be endured with as little inconvenience as possible. One suspects, however, that the real result was that those who held those views kept their religious faith in a special compartment separated from the ordinary affairs of life, and that in consequence there arose an inconsistency between a religious profession of undoubted sincerity and the failure to express it in the supposedly secular occupations and interests of the world. This brought upon formal religion and those who practised it a condemnation which it can hardly be denied was often deserved.

The event which shattered this complacency once and for all was the first World War, when the scandal of nominally Christian nations engaged in slaughtering one another on a vast scale produced a reaction which found expression in the Copec Conference (Conference on Politics, Economies, and Citizenship) of 1924. From then onwards the gospel began to be proclaimed primarily in its social implications, and scores of books were written and sermons preached on 'Christianity and International Relations', 'Christianity and Industry', and so forth, the effect of which was to make man fall into the opposite error of considering this life as an end in itself and of concentrating all attention and endeavour on the estab-lishment of the Kingdom of God on earth. This is an expression in a Christian context of the avowed Com-munist aim of regarding the be-all and end-all of human history as the establishment of the perfect Communist classless society. Either goal is portrayed as one which, when achieved, will prove to have justified all the struggles and sufferings of endless generations of the human race.

But, as so often happens, the pendulum has swung too far. The truth is that otherworldliness and thisworldliness are alike inadequate by themselves. They need each other if they are to be kept in proper balance. Together they afford a worthy and satisfying philosophy of life for men and women made in the image of God.

If men are just machines, wound up but gradually slowing down, or animals to be made as comfortable as possible during their short life and then painlessly put out of the way, it might properly be argued that truth is still truth and goodness still goodness; it would still be better to be generous than mean, and kind rather than cruel. But these values, though valid, would be but temporary and unrelated to anything ultimate or eternal. As far as we are concerned, it will be all the same in a hundred years time whether we have been good or bad. Similarly, a social order where men live together in happiness and peace would be greatly to be desired, but again of only temporary importance. But if, on the other hand, this life is only a porch, leading to a fuller life, if man himself is an immortal soul with a place in God's eternal purpose, if his destiny hereafter depends in any sense on how that purpose is fulfilled or thwarted here, if his membership of the human family is a foretaste of his membership of the redeemed family of God in heaven, the picture is transformed and earthly things assume a new and vital importance, not in contrast to heavenly things, but because of them. It is belief in eternity which alone invests the things of time with their real significance.

At this point the doctrine of Christian perfection reinforces the doctrine of immortality. There is something in man that craves perfection, a divine discontent that can never be satisfied with less than the best. That is true in relatively small things like the arrangement of flowers or the construction of aeroplanes; but it is supremely true in the moral sphere. The sky's the limit there as elsewhere. Nothing so destroys the fibre of character as contentment with oneself. It was the besetting sin of the Pharisee. He had gone a long way. The trouble was that he believed he had arrived; there was nowhere else to go. It is no accident that the greatest saints are those most conscious of their sin; this is part of man's greatness. Across the path of his progress looms the inevitability of death. With animals it is not so. The animal can be satisfied in a sense which is impossible for a man. It is without reasoning faculty or imagination, and so death holds no terrors for it. It has been remarked that the possession of one idea, the idea of death, would raise an animal to the status of a man.

Far from the idea of immortality being irrational, it can be maintained that the really irrational thing would be if man with his superb intelligence, his power of reasoning, his ability to recognize and seek after the true, the beautiful, and the good, could be blotted out by a microbe or a bomb. He would then be a permanent misfit in a universe where he had been encouraged to foster desires out of harmony with reality. He would be reduced to explaining the nature of reality in terms lower than himself. Ultimate defect and disillusionment would be his fate. So also the social aspirations which at least from the time of Plato have inspired successive generations of mankind would need to be written off and might almost as well be abandoned. Why strive unceasingly when disappointment and frustration are all that can be expected?

But can this be the truth? Things have not so turned out in other respects. The desires man shares with animals for food and love are desires which are capable of being satisfied. It would be the height of irony if this desire peculiar to man, the desire for perfection, were doomed to final frustration. In the scientific world when some secret which has remained hidden from the beginning of time is finally revealed, the reality is invariably more wonderful than man in his wildest flight of imagination has dared to guess. Must it not so prove in this most mysterious realm of all, the destiny of human personality? Or are we to resign ourselves to the idea of the universe as a bad joke after all?

In this respect it is the doctrine of Christian perfection which reinforces the doctrine of immortality, while the doctrine of immortality in its turn affords the only adequate setting for the doctrine of perfection.

Before passing on, mention should be made of the spiritualists, who are at the opposite extreme to the rationalists in that they affirm that life continues in the hereafter and claim to prove it by evidence. Most spiritualists are sincere and earnest people and everyone recognizes the poignant facts of human experience which lead men to turn to spiritualism for consolation. Moreover, it would be quite wrong to discourage any kind of research which is reverently and honestly conducted. It must be pointed out, however, that from the point of view of our present inquiry the claims they make, even if they were established, would be irrelevant. For if I understand them aright, their concern is to prove the fact of survival. But that is not the same thing as the Christian doctrine of immortality. Most spiritualists do in fact believe in the existence of God, but I see no reason why they must do so, any more than people who believe in the 'here and now' need believe in God in consequence. Belief in survival, though interesting, is not of itself a religious belief at all. And it must be confessed that the distressing feature of their claims, as the late Professor A. E. Taylor remarked, is that the life they profess to disclose would not be a life nearer to God, the fountain of wisdom and goodness. The supposed utterances of men who were wise and virtuous while they were among us do not suggest they are wiser and more virtuous now that they have left our company, but often grotesquely otherwise. Without pronouncing on the validity of these revelations, we may say that any belief which puts survival first, and estimates that prospect independently of God's character and purpose, is a poor substitute for Christian truth, which is concerned not so much with the fact of life hereafter as with its quality and man's glorious destiny as a child of God.

Let us consider this further in the light of the perpetual tension between time and eternity which exists in human life. No fact more persistently intrudes upon our consciousness, especially as we grow older, than the fact of time. The ninetieth Psalm finds an echo in all our hearts: 'We spend our years as a tale that is told.' We are conscious of the relentless process of time with which so many of the good things we enjoy are bound up. Things we could once do we can do no longer. Each day and each period brings with it its own good which must be appropriated in its due season or not at all. The wonder and divine thoughtlessness of childhood give way to the ardour and impetuosity of youth. This in time yields to the life, wisdom, and assured judgement of mature manhood. Finally comes the reflective serenity which should characterize old age. The point is that these good things are not cumulative. Each of them has to be relinquished in order that the succeeding good may be enjoyed. We are often reluctant to let go, and there ensues the sorry spectacle always presented when men or women attempt to behave as if they were much younger than they really are. In spite of the whimsical genius of J. M. Barrie, Peter Pan, the boy who wouldn't grow up, is a deplorable character.

Similarly, with the changing pattern of developing communities, we who live in the reign of Queen Elizabeth II inhabit a very different England from that of Elizabeth I. We enjoy the blessings of the Welfare State, and blessings I hold them to be. Yet it is idle not to recognize that the social security of the present age has been won at the cost of opportunities for initiative and adventure which were available in former days. We cannot enjoy the benefits of socialism and at the same time retain the benefits of private enterprise. Viewing the international scene, it would appear that the only prospect of a happy future for mankind lies in some form of world government. Nationalism, which in its day marked a great advance on the system it supplanted, has had its day and no longer meets the needs of men. But nations are naturally hesitant about abandoning one jot or tittle of their absolute sovereignty. Yet the plunge must be taken if the world, which has shrunk in a generation to the dimensions of a neighbourhood, is to realize the immense possibilities of the new age which is dawning. Thus for individuals and for society the satisfactions and the disappointments of life are fleeting. With everything else they are borne away on the stream of time.

But while the truth of this, however unpalatable we may find it, seems obvious and beyond dispute, it is not the whole truth. We belong to time which has us in its grip but not entirely so. In addition to the good things belonging to the successive stages of our pilgrimage which may be enjoyed but for a time, there is some good to be realized that does not become obsolete. It resides in what is usually called character or, as I would rather put it, in the people we are in process of becoming. For by far the most important thing that is happening to us as we live our lives is that each of us is becoming a certain kind of person, and what matters more than anything else is what kind of person that is. We recognize this when we say that, however we may feel at the moment, the important thing is never what happens to us but how we react to whatever happens. We are not finished products but are in process of becoming. And in this respect the principle is cumulative. We have become the people we are today because of what we have been in all our yesterdays. If I look back twenty years and visualize myself as I was twenty years ago, I realize that I am a different person.

Physically, so I am informed, I have changed about three times during that period, but a corresponding mental and spiritual change has been taking place all the time. And yet it is myself twenty years ago that I visualize and not somebody else. Amid all the development and change there has been a continuing identity, the reality of which I am conscious of through the faculty of memory. This factor of identity has defied the ravages of time which have swept away so much. Similarly, though it may be harder to define, a nation or any other community can retain and develop characteristics through all the vicissitudes of fortune. For individuals and for society the past is gathered up into the present and leads to the future, and the conclusion of all this is not in time; it is independent of time and belongs to eternity.

If this is so, as I believe it to be, it follows that belief in eternity does not diminish, but immeasurably enhances, the significance of the things of time. For those things become a kind of trellis work on which a plant may be trained which will abide when the trellis work is no more. The experiences of time, the joys and the sorrows, the successes and the failure, provide the stuff out of which eternal values are forged. I shall be a better husband, a better craftsman, a better citizen of my earthly country if I believe that I am destined for eternal life, than if the transient goods of time are all I can ever hope to enjoy. The incentive to build the Kingdom of God on earth becomes not weaker, but infinitely stronger, if we believe that Kingdom to be not merely a static and necessarily temporary earthly goal but a pattern in time of the eternal Kingdom of God in heaven.

But some may say, All this is vague and indefinite; after all, time is real but eternity is at best only a surmise. On the contrary, the exact opposite is the truth. Whatever doubts may be entertained about eternity, time beyond all question is relative and not absolute. It is a good many years ago that the French romantic novelist, Jules Verne, wrote *Round the World in Eighty Days*, the story of Mr Phileas Fogg who made a bet in his London club that he would circle the globe within the space of eighty days and arrive back again. After a series of breath-taking adventures he believed that he had just lost his bet, but he had overlooked the vital fact that by travelling in an easterly direction he had saved a day. Although he had seen the sun set and rise again eighty times, his friends in London had only witnessed that event seventy-nine times, and he had won his wager after all. This fact about time is much more obvious in these days of air travel, when two or three days at the most would suffice and watches would need to be constantly adjusted. Time depends on nothing fixed, but on movement in space, and is bound up with matter which perishes. We can appreciate better perhaps than the New Testament writer himself his prophecy that 'There shall be time no longer'. Time is running out. One day it will be no more. Even here, as creatures of time, in our experiences we can sometimes become independent of it. 'Though our outward man is decaying, yet our inward man is renewed day by day.' The good things of time come and go, but God's eternal purpose of good for us is being worked out 'while we look not at the things which are seen, but at the things which are not seen: for the things which are seen are temporal; but the things which are not seen are eternal'. Half an hour in a dentist's chair may indeed seem an eternity, but a whole evening at a New Year Party is gone in a flash. And in our deepest experiences, too, time has no meaning. A symphony concert, though it be one movement after another in succession, brings a message to us that has nothing to do with time; and so do friendship and love. In these ways our lives are shot through with anticipations of eternity.

For those who hold the Christian faith, the supreme ground of our conviction is our interpretation of the meaning of the events in history which gave rise to that faith.

Nineteen hundred years ago eternity entered into time; God became Man. His life on earth had a beginning at Bethlehem and it had an end on Calvary. Between these events He was subject, as we are, to time, and time did its worst with Him. All the evil things in time were mobilized against Him, and when time won what seemed its final triumph over Him and His days on earth were abruptly ended, it was He who really conquered. While in the flesh He displayed the goodness and love of God amid things of time, and ever since His power has been actively at work, meeting and overcoming the evil in men's hearts and in the world.

To hold that God's supreme strategy in the Incarnation should have as its goal the reconciliation of man to God for the few brief years of his earthly existence is about as reasonable as to try to stand a pyramid on its point. That the love which took Him to the cross that we might be forgiven and redeemed should be so restricted in its scope is an incredible thought, contrary alike to reason and to our Lord's oft repeated promises. Equally incredible is it that the salvation He offers should fall short of the perfection He enjoined. In both these respects we may ask with John Newton—

> *And can He have taught me*
> *To trust in His name*
> *And thus far have brought me*
> *To put me to shame?*

Eternity entered into time that we who live in time might know that we belong to eternity. He lived our life that we might live His; and if we respond to His love, His power is ours here and now so that we too may win the victory over all that mars and degrades our manhood and finally, when time says the final word to us on earth, we shall be released from the narrow confines of this life and enter into the life of perfect love in the family of God.

CHAPTER XI

THE CHURCH

IN an earlier section of this book we noted the essentially social nature of man. We are always individuals, but never merely individual. From the beginning we grow up in a social context. We are nurtured by parents, taught and disciplined at home and in school, and finally take our place as adult citizens of a community. It is generally recognized that any man who attempts to contract out of this many-sided relationship is to that extent revealing some defect in his personality. Life has little meaning if a man lives it in isolation, and right behaviour involves right relationship with other people.

This is true if we confine our consideration to so-called secular relationships, but it is doubly true if we bring religion into it, for while religion is always personal, it is never private. 'The New Testament', John Wesley declared, 'knows nothing of a solitary religion.' And again, 'there is no holiness except social holiness'. The perfection which is God's purpose for us is perfect love, and perfect love involves someone other than ourselves. It is love to God and love to man, and these are not distinct and separate things, but two aspects of the same thing. This is the answer to those people we come across every now and then who maintain that they can be better disciples of Jesus on their own than by linking up with a Church. Such an attitude betrays a complete misunderstanding of the nature of man and of the Christian religion. On our part, the Christian life begins when we make a response to Jesus who died for us and calls us to be His disciples. But by that very response we come into a new relationship to the great company of men and women of every race and colour who have made the same response. In this respect the Church resembles a family rather than an institution, that is to say, it is a natural rather than an artificial organization. Men who have interests they share with others, or some common object in view, form clubs or societies to foster those interests or achieve those objects, but they do so of their own volition and are free to abandon them at any time. But it is not so with the family. We do not choose our parents, nor our brothers and sisters in the home; there they are and we accept them. The Christian Church is like that. When we respond to the love of God in Jesus, by that very act, without the need of any subsequent decision, we become part of the family of God. We are each of us bound to our Lord by His love, but that same bond binds Him to all His followers and binds them to each other. It may be disconcerting but it is true, and in point of fact it is a most thrilling thing, for it means belonging to the only family of its kind that the world has ever known, one that knows no boundaries and includes men and women of every sort and kind.

These are the basic spiritual principles on which the Christian Church rests: our relationship to Jesus as Saviour and Lord and our relationship to one another as members of the redeemed family. Buildings, creeds, forms of service, and the rest, all the paraphernalia that necessarily belong to an institution, are the superstructure, not the foundation; though it is of these things that people within the Church and outside it first think when the Church is mentioned, and it is on these matters that disputes arise and attempts at unity break down. It is the mutual love of Christians for each other which is the mark of true discipleship of the Master: 'By this shall all men know that ye are my disciples if ye have love one to another.'

The Church is not composed of men and women who

are already perfect. It is the company of those who have said 'yes' to God in Jesus Christ and are being saved. The biggest factor in that process is the gracious work of the Holy Spirit in our hearts, and we rightly insist in the Protestant tradition on the direct accessibility of God to every contrite human spirit. 'When thou prayest, enter into thine inner chamber, and having shut thy door, pray to thy Father which is in secret, and thy Father which seeth in secret shall recompense thee.' But the next most fruitful means whereby the grace of God is mediated to us is through each other. This is a truth which Methodists above all people should know, for it was the way in which Methodism spread. We were societies long before we were congregations, let alone churches, and if we have lost our hold in the last fifty years, as we must all admit that in a measure we have, the neglect of this our traditional and distinctive means of grace has been a big contributory factor. Meanwhile it is significant that not only has the method of group fellowship been discovered and employed by certain other Christian organizations to their great benefit, but the most vital and hopeful revival within our own denomination, namely, the Methodist societies in the Universities and Colleges, is largely built upon it. It is my conviction that any large-scale revival within Methodism will spring from and be nurtured by a renewal of what is our characteristic spiritual activity. It is no exaggeration to say that, whatever any notice board may declare to the contrary, no church is in the full sense a Methodist church where there are no regular meetings for fellowship. For, while the new relationship in which every pledged disciple of Jesus automatically finds himself knows no frontiers and is world wide, it is within the intimacy of the worshipping community at a particular place that Christian fellowship is richest. Above all, it is there that the mutual love which is the true mark of Christian discipleship can be demonstrated.

'Love one another' is the command of our Lord to all His disciples, but though the opportunities for such action towards our brethren in distant lands are limited, every local community calling itself a Christian church, however ineffective it is sometimes tempted to think its witness must be, has in fact the power to demonstrate in its own life and fellowship what the whole world will be like when the whole world accepts the Lordship of Jesus Christ which that small community professes. If we fail there, it is idle to lament that in wider spheres men ignore us and do not heed our message. If, for example, we are unable in a spirit of love to resolve our own domestic differences, how can we sincerely proclaim the gospel of reconciliation?

Furthermore, the perfection which God wills to bestow on the individual believer is a perfection which He also intends shall characterize the worshipping community. Consciously or unconsciously we acknowledge this every time we sing Charles Wesley's best-known hymn of Christian fellowship:

> *Christ, from whom all blessings flow*
> *Perfecting the saints below.*

In this connexion let us recall the letter to the Ephesians, which is generally regarded as being in fact a circular letter to several of the young Christian communities: '. . . Christ also loved the church and gave Himself up for it: that He might sanctify it . . . that He might present the church to himself a glorious church, not having spot or wrinkle or any such thing; but that it should be holy and without blemish.' Or let us recall the first epistle of Peter, one of what are called the catholic epistles, because they were addressed not to one particular local church, but to churches in general: 'We also, as living stones, are built up a spiritual house, to be a holy priesthood.' Or again: 'Ye are an elect race, a royal priesthood, a holy nation, a people for God's own possession, that ye may shew forth the excellences of him who called you out of darkness into his marvellous light.'

While such passages often rebuke us when we relate them to our own local church, they seem to me to have something to say to us also about the scandal of the disunity between the Churches. I have already referred to the fact that no one who is familiar with the origins of the different denominations would regard our denominational differences as wholly sinful. The fact remains that in the context of the present world situation they do constitute a stumbling block, which is what the word 'scandal' historically implies.

This is nowhere more apparent than when we come to consider the other relationship in which the Church stands, namely its relationship to the outside world. We have been discussing the relationship of mutual love which is the true mark of the community of Christian disciples. But of equal importance is the responsibility which membership of that community involves in relation to the bigger community, the whole family of God, which includes all men everywhere. 'God so loved' not the Church but 'the world', and Jesus came to save the world. In the world the Church is the visible community of those who are being saved, and together the holy universal Church is committed to the evangelization of all men. If we are reconciled to God through Jesus Christ we are restored to that desire to co-operate with Him and be the instruments of His holy will for all mankind. Unto us is committed the ministry of reconciliation. We are to be to others what Christ has been to us.

This is the task which is usually summed up in the word 'evangelism', but we must beware of the danger of allowing that word to become a technical term, reserved for one special form of activity and thereby robbed of some of its scope and significance. Every individual believer is charged with this responsibility at every point at which he touches life, but, important as our individual witness may be, the task can only be effectively faced by the whole Christian community acting in co-operation, for it is the whole of human life which needs redeeming. In the words of Dr George Macleod, God, revealed in Jesus Christ, is 'the At-one-ment between the Godhead and the True Community, but not in any ethereal sense of an isolated worshipping Community but of a total Community of Body and Soul. He cannot be found except in community nor can community be found except in Him.'

The weakness of much current evangelism is not in what it does but in what it omits to do. It is quite hopeless to approach the problems of evangelism on the principle that the first step is to win men and women individually to allegiance to Jesus, and that the working out of the implications of Christianity for the various spheres of community life follows afterwards. The first step would also prove to be the only step. What we call 'the implications', as if they were purely secondary and consequential, are in fact as much the proper field of evangelism as is the individual who needs salvation. In the world today it is at these levels that the eternal truths of the Gospel are most likely to come alive for men. Happily there are a number of signs that in our own Church and in others a more adequate ground-plan of evangelism is being thought out. Mention need only be made of the development in Britain of industrial chaplaincies, and in the international field of the work of the Churches Commission on International Affairs, where Christian influence is being brought to bear in a truly remarkable way wherever statesmen gather to deal with urgent and dangerous situations. In our own Church the Home Mission Department and the Youth Department bring home to us something of the many-sided nature of Methodist evangelistic enterprise, though we do not always realize that the Christian Citizenship Department is equally concerned with the preaching of the Gospel, but tend to regard it as only a subsidiary activity. We need to keep ever in mind the words of Isaiah which our Lord made His own manifesto at the outset of His ministry:

The Spirit of the Lord is upon me,
Because he anointed me to preach good tidings to the poor:
He hath sent me to proclaim release to the captives,
And recovering of sight to the blind,
To set at liberty them that are bruised,
To proclaim the acceptable year of the Lord.

While it is obvious that with the best will in the world the reunion of Churches will inevitably be a slow process, what one feels might happen and what surely should happen is the same active co-operation at the level of the local church as is taking place increasingly at the national and international level. In every village, town, and suburb the conflict between good and evil proceeds. Wherever men live in homes, work in factories, shops and offices, and engage in multifarious social activities, God and the devil are in rivalry for the souls of men and for the allegiance of the community. What a transformation would be effected if those who bear the name of Jesus, though still worshipping in their own buildings and cherishing their own traditions, were nevertheless avowedly and actively on the same side in these vital matters, welcoming each other as allies and effectively united for practical action. For together this responsibility is assuredly theirs, and the more they truly worship God and the more holy they become, the more they will feel committed to their common task. The love that binds them to their Lord is the Love that binds them to each other, and is the Love that gives itself utterly for every child of God, and every part of His family.

But that is not the whole of it. The Church is universal not only in extent but in depth. It transcends not only all earthly barriers, as we have seen, but the greatest barrier of all, the barrier of death. That is what is meant when the Church is described as 'militant on earth, triumphant in heaven'. We are all familiar with the New Testament metaphor of the Christian life as a pilgrimage. We are running a race, finishing a course. Round the ropes that mark off the track is the 'cloud of witnesses' who have already run the race and finished the course. The visible community of Christians round about us is just a small fraction of the redeemed society in the making. We cannot limit our thought of the Church within the narrow frontiers of this world's life. Those who have gone before us in the faith have gone to another world, but not to another Church.

Nowhere, as far as I know, is this faith better illustrated than in Charles Wesley's hymn 'Come let us join our friends above'—

> One family we dwell in Him,
>   One Church, above, beneath,
> Though now divided by the stream,
>   The narrow stream of death:
> One army of the living God,
>   To His command we bow;
> Part of His host have crossed the flood,
>   And part are crossing now.

The reality of this is brought home to us at every Communion service when 'with angels and archangels and all the company of heaven' we glorify God's holy name.

We have already considered at length how the doctrine of immortality affords the only adequate setting for the doctrine of Christian perfection.

It remains only to suggest—and as 'we walk by faith not by sight', we can do no more than suggest—some possible implications of the doctrine of the communion of saints in this respect. Here we are in the field of speculation, but it is permissible to speculate if we do so reverently and if our speculation is consistent with the character of God revealed in Jesus Christ.

We believe that when we respond to the love of God in Jesus, the Holy Spirit begins His work of transforming grace in our hearts, which will only be completed when He has made us perfect. But quite obviously in many sincere Christians that process is never completed on earth. What then? The physical act of dying contains no moral dynamic. Furthermore, it is essential to our belief that it should be those same people and not other people who survive death. People die in various states and at various times, some in infancy, some in war, some at a ripe old age. Some have had many chances, some never, it would seem, a fair chance. To meet such difficulties the Roman Catholic Church has its doctrine of Purgatory, an intermediate state between this world and heaven where redeemed souls go until they are fit for the bliss of heaven. This doctrine has been mixed up with ideas of merit, with the practice of indulgences, and is altogether repugnant to the Protestant mind. The Reformers rejected it and, rightly insisting that salvation is by faith alone, taught that the redeemed soul goes straight to heaven. But thereby they created other difficulties as we have seen. It would appear that in our thinking, room must be left for the continuance of the redemptive activity of God in Jesus Christ, a belief which can surely be held quite apart from the offensive aspects of the traditional Roman doctrine of Purgatory. What Jesus revealed for a few years on the stage of history was not some temporary phenomenon, but God's eternal attitude. As He loved us before we were born, we are surely in His just and loving keeping after we die. And as the perfection He proposes for us is to be enjoyed within the redeemed family, it may well be that the doctrine of the communion of saints is relevant to this. In the famous eleventh chapter of Hebrews, the heroes of days gone by, Gideon, Samson, Barak, and the rest are linked with the Christian saints of later days, 'God having provided some better thing concerning us that they without us should not be made perfect'. It is surely not fanciful to see a hint here that, in the timeless order of God's eternal world, undeveloped souls may draw on the treasury of life of succeeding generations and fulfil their destiny in the wider community and the unrestricted fellowship of God's other world.

Whether the Church triumphant will finally include everybody we do not know. It is never definitely so stated in the New Testament where the weight of evidence would tend on balance to be against universalism. If we hold the view that all will in the end be saved, that faith must rest not on any specific New Testament word, but on trust in the final victory of the love of God for all men as revealed in Jesus Christ.

All speculation is of course made difficult because we are trying to imagine and describe eternity in language that belongs to space and time. What we can be assured of is that the life hereafter will be a life of perfect love, where our personalities will be enriched and fulfilled in the heavenly community, the eternal family of God, where He, Creator, Redeemer, and Perfecter, is all in all.

CHAPTER XII

THE HOLY SPIRIT

WHEN the bodily presence of our Lord was finally withdrawn from His disciples on the occasion we call the Ascension, they rapidly made two discoveries. The first of them took place on the Day of Pentecost, when they realized that although no longer with them in the flesh, Jesus was with them in an even more effective way through the presence of the Holy Spirit in their hearts. During His earthly life He had promised that this would be so. 'It is expedient for you', He said, 'that I go away: for if I go not away, the Comforter will not come unto you; but if I go, I will send him unto you.' At the time they had been unable to understand His meaning, but they understood it now. No longer did they depend upon His external presence. They were aware of His power at work within and through them.

The second discovery was in its results even more remarkable. As the first messengers of the Gospel made their way outside the narrow confines of the Holy Land, where the events had taken place which gave rise to their new faith, into the countries of Europe and Asia Minor around the Eastern Mediterranean, they found that wherever they told the story of what the love of God had done in Jesus, if the people who heard it responded with believing hearts, the same miracle took place, and these men and women, although they themselves had neither seen Jesus nor heard Him speak, entered into the same experience and came to know Him as Saviour and Lord. And so it has continued through the centuries. The Christian message has spanned continents and oceans.

Neither lapse of time nor distance of space has diminished its power. This is the work of the Holy Spirit.

Thus the late Archbishop William Temple described the Holy Spirit as 'first and foremost the special and distinctive influence which God exerts over our souls as we respond to His love in the human life of Christ'.

The Holy Spirit is God. He is not an attribute of God, but God Himself. There is only one God. The invisible eternal Being, who made all things, is the Divine Spirit who speaks in our hearts. On the stage of history God appeared, and men received a knowledge of Him which could only be given in the fashion of a human life. As Jesus was in time, God always has been and always will be. Since Jesus came, there has been a new content in men's thoughts of God the Creator and Sustainer of the universe, and of God the Holy Spirit at work in men's minds and hearts. The Holy Spirit is the Love wherewith the Son loves the Father and the Father loves the Son. He also is the love wherewith a man loves God or his brother man. He is the ground and bond of the fellowship which binds us to Himself and to one another.

In formal theological statements this is set forth in what is known as the Doctrine of the Trinity in which Christian thinkers have sought to piece together all we know about God from different sources. In the language of experience it is not always possible to distinguish the Persons of the Godhead in so clear-cut a manner. This need not alarm us. It would be surprising if we, with our finite minds of limited range, could so define the eternal Godhead. So Paul can write: 'Now the Lord is the Spirit: and where the Spirit of the Lord is, there is liberty'; and Charles Wesley, who wrote so many hymns about the Holy Spirit, wrote an equal number in which the transforming and redeeming activity of God is attributed to the risen Lord; and Christians everywhere constantly refer to the Second and Third Persons of the Trinity as though they were interchangeable in this respect. And why not? For Jesus is the source of the Holy Spirit in us. To quote William Temple again: 'Into our lives, as in the Being of the Godhead, the Holy Spirit proceeds not only from the Father, but from the Father through the Son.'

The important thing to recognize is that it is through the life of the Holy Spirit that the life of the Church through the Ages has been maintained, and that the historic events which took place in Palestine nineteen hundred years ago were no passing episode but the revelation in time of the eternal Love of God which is for ever active in the world and redemptive in the souls of men. Otherwise we might look back across the centuries to Jesus as the supreme example to mankind for all time, but we could not adore Him as our present Saviour and Lord.

I do not believe it to be an exaggeration to claim that no revival of Christian life can more appropriately be described as a movement of the Spirit than the Methodist revival in the eighteenth century and its subsequent expansion throughout this country and across the world. To this the Doctrine of Assurance, which expressed the joyous experience of those who, as they gave themselves to Jesus, knew their sins to be forgiven and became aware of new power released within them, bears eloquent testimony. Marvellous as this experience was and still can be, let us not regard it as some mysterious and mystical happening beyond any possible understanding.

Much unnecessary confusion has been caused in men's thinking about the Holy Spirit by the association of His activity mainly with abnormal occurrences. It is true that when the disciples first became conscious of His presence there was an outbreak of intense emotional excitement; it was only to be expected that it should be so; nor is the story at Pentecost an isolated instance in this respect. But by contrast, how naturally Jesus speaks in this connexion: any decent human father, whatever his faults,

will give his son bread or fish, the basic provision for the
material needs of every day; so, our Heavenly Father will
supply the spiritual needs of His children when they ask
Him.

The Holy Spirit, being God, is personal. He is much
greater than any individual person we have ever known,
but He is personal, and the relationship between Him and
us can best be understood in personal terms. That is how
Jesus taught us to think about God. Now in ordinary life
the strongest influence determining for good or evil what
kind of people we are becoming is the influence not of
ideas but of persons. No man liveth unto himself; everybody influences us and we influence everybody we meet.
How differently we behave in the company of some
people from the way in which we are liable to behave in
the company of some other people. Our personalities are
not isolated; we are so made that the presence of somebody we care about and to whom we respond can bring
to us an inflow of life and vital energy. This is the explanation of how any football team will play better if led and
inspired by a captain they trust; it accounts for the difference in a man or woman when they fall in love; it is set
forth in popular song and common story and needs no
elaborate exposition. It is the power that only a person
can exert, and it is the key to understanding the secret
that lies at the heart of Christianity. For Christianity
confronts the world not primarily with a creed to be
believed nor a code of behaviour to be observed, but with
a Person to be followed. The crucial decision is with our
wills. It is not within our own power to save ourselves.
Selfish people cannot make themselves unselfish nor evil
people make themselves good; these are things that only
God can do. What we can decide is whether or not we
are going to allow Him to influence us. Are we going to
allow Him to bring our wills into harmony with His
divine will? Many people are unwilling to make this

submission. They feel that there is something derogatory to true manhood in it. But our wills cannot be self-directing in a kind of vacuum. If not surrendered to God they will be in bondage to some less worthy ideal, or at best at the mercy of every passing whim of our own. It is as we offer them to Him that they become really ours.

> Our wills are ours, we know not how;
> Our wills are ours, to make them Thine.

When that has happened, the Holy Spirit carries on the work of grace in our hearts and we can say in Paul's words, which seem to me to sum up the Christian experience better than any other, 'I live and yet no longer I. Christ liveth in me.'

This is the work of the Holy Spirit, but what is the bearing on it of the Doctrine of Christian Perfection, which we are especially considering? Surely this. The Christian disciple is freed once and for all from subservience to even the highest code, but His whole life is now guided by a limitless principle, the principle of perfect love, in following which He is dependent not on his own strength, which would be utterly unequal to the demand, but on the power of the Holy Spirit who is Almighty.

When Jesus came and showed men once and for all how life should be lived, He came to a people who already possessed in their law the loftiest code of behaviour yet devised, of which the scribes and Pharisees were the acknowledged exponents and guardians. He swept away as not good enough the best that men had known: 'Except your righteousness shall exceed the righteousness of the scribes and Pharisees, ye shall in no wise enter into the kingdom of heaven.' Instead He substituted the demand for perfection, exceeding in its limitless requirement the highest external standard.

When in answer to Peter's inquiry about the limits of forgiveness our Lord replied, 'I say not unto thee "until seven times", but "until seventy times seven" ', He was substituting for the most that could reasonably be expected of a generous man a counsel of perfection. Yet this same Jesus is recorded by the same evangelist as saying: 'Come unto me, all ye that labour and are heavy laden, and I will give you rest. Take my yoke upon you, and learn of me; for I am meek and lowly in heart: and ye shall find rest unto your souls. For my yoke is easy, and my burden is light.'

Here is a paradox indeed. Its explanation takes us to the heart of our Christian faith. Rules are essential for law and order in a community, and can be a great assistance in the ordering of our individual lives so long as they are not elevated to an absolute level, in which event we either fail to observe them and are in despair, or succeed in observing them and like the Pharisee are in the even more perilous state of complacency. There is all the difference in the world between a set of rules we accept and set ourselves to attain by our own efforts, and a personal relationship the limitless consequence of which we joyfully explore and increasingly realize. Paul, the conscientious Pharisee, eager to do everything possible to fulfil every jot and tittle of the law, is frustrated and miserable. Paul, the converted Christian, no longer under the law but faced with the absolute demands of the Christian disciple, is at peace and radiates joy.

Conscientiousness is a necessary and admirable virtue, but it is different from and less than the Christian religion. There is no need to be a Christian to be conscientious. All sorts of people, Jews, Mohammedans, and indeed atheists, often display the virtue of conscientiousness. The trouble is that for many genuinely sincere and devoted people Christian discipleship is a higher form of conscientiousness with the ethic of Jesus taking the place of other inferior standards. The effect of this is that their Christian faith has simply brought an additional burden and one which will in the end prove insupportable. It is as if a man tried to push up a hill the car which was intended to carry him. The heart of the Gospel is that what we can neither achieve nor earn, what cannot be bought and what we do not deserve, God in His infinite mercy offers to us as a gift. The gift is communicated through the Holy Spirit and is the direct result of our response to the Love of God revealed to us in the life and death of Jesus Christ.

The Jesus of history becomes our great contemporary. He becomes a fact of our own consciences and challenges us. We cannot imitate Him, but we can allow Him to influence us. Above all, we can worship Him who alone is worthy of the adoration of our whole beings. And as in glad and free surrender we place Him in the centre of our hearts and thoughts, lesser loyalties fall into their rightful place, and our lives take on a new pattern. No, we cannot imitate Him, but we can be made like Him. Let Paul describe what the end shall be when He shall have wrought in us His perfect work. 'We all, . . . reflecting as a mirror the glory of the Lord, are transformed into the same image from glory to glory.'

CHAPTER XIII

THE FAITH OF A METHODIST

I HAVE often felt on occasions when I have been engaged in conversation with fellow Christians of other communions the need of a succinct statement summarizing our distinctive Methodist emphases. 'You are a Methodist', says some casual acquaintance. 'What exactly does that involve? How are you different from other kinds of Christians?'

It is easy to reassure him as to our rightful place in the universal Church by telling him what we have in common with others, such as our acceptance of the historic creeds, but he is not usually interested in that. He wants to know what is distinctive about us.

We have no creed that belongs to us alone and I am sure it would be a great mistake to attempt to frame one. We have an admirable catechism, but it is far too long to be of service in this particular way, and quite unsuitable for the purpose anyhow.

But there is in our hymn-book a hymn of Charles Wesley, containing only two stanzas, which in that brief compass appears to me to meet every requirement. Unlike many of Charles Wesley's hymns in their present form, it does not consist of various verses extracted from a long poem, but has been complete in itself from the beginning. It deals with the grace of God in the individual soul and needs to be supplemented, if it is desired to include the social aspect of our Faith, but with that reservation it is flawless and complete. Let us consider it couplet by couplet.

Jesus, the First and Last,
On Thee my soul is cast.

The hymn opens by directing our thoughts and prayers to Jesus. That is the only place to begin. Methodism, like the whole of the Christian religion, is the fruit of man's response to God's initiative. Christianity did not originate in anything that good or clever men have thought as they have reflected on the Universe round about them or on their own experience, but in what God did nineteen hundred years ago. For every individual the Christian life begins when, having neither merit nor hope in himself, he casts himself in faith on God, who has loved him and sought him in Jesus Christ. This Jesus, who was born at Bethlehem and died on Calvary, is the eternal Son of God. He is the First and the Last: 'In him were all things created, in the heavens and upon the earth, things visible and things invisible, whether thrones or dominions or principalities or powers; all things have been created through him, and unto him; and he is before all things, and in him all things consist.' As the past has been His, the future also is His: 'For he must reign, till he hath put all his enemies under his feet. And when all things have been subjected unto him, then shall the Son also himself be subjected to him that did subject all things unto him, that God may be all in all.'

Thou didst Thy work begin
By blotting out my sin.

That is the first thing Jesus does for us, because it is the first thing we need. Before the transforming work of grace can begin in our hearts, we need forgiveness and the restoration of the broken relationship to God which our sins have brought about.

> *Thou wilt the root remove*
> *And perfect me in love.*

But forgiveness of the actual sins we have committed is only the first step in a process, during which a radical change takes place in our personalities. The sins we have committed are serious, but much more serious is the sinful state of which they were the expression. It is we ourselves, the people we really are, who need to be changed by the grace of God into the people He intends us to become. That transforming work, which begins when, in whatever state we are, we cast ourselves in faith on the love of Jesus, never ends until His perfect work is completed in love.

Then comes the second stanza.

> *Yet when the work is done,*
> *The work is but begun.*

That is sheer religious genius, and shows us Charles Wesley at his best and most characteristic. It may appear illogical, but like a somewhat similar line 'For ever beginning what never shall end', which could have been written by nobody else, it reveals rare spiritual insight. There is a sense in which 'the work is done'; as Philip Doddridge, another hymn-writer of the eighteenth century, wrote, ''Tis done, the great transaction's done'. There is a sense in which it is possible for us through Jesus Christ to enter once and for all into a new relationship with God. Everything will be different for ever afterwards. And yet anyone who knows his own heart realizes full well that it has to be done again and again, and the glory of the Gospel is that there can be innumerable new beginnings. Charles Wesley came to realize the necessity of this. 'A gracious soul may fall from grace.' And, moreover, the path to perfection resembles the climbing of a mountain. The heights we scale prove not to be the summit, but the starting-point for a fresh ascent to peaks not seen before.

> *Partaker of Thy grace,*
> *I long to see Thy face.*

Charles Wesley never wanders far from the Scriptures, and here we have an echo of the great New Testament word, 'Beloved, now are we children of God, and it is not yet made manifest what we shall be. We know that, if he shall be manifested, we shall be like him; for we shall see him even as he is.' So present experience is linked with future hope. Such is the scope of the transformation we need, which we are promised His grace and power will finally effect, and the reward is the vision of God to those who are made like Him and pure in heart.

> *The first I prove below,*
> *The last I die to know.*

Through the love of God we are given a place in His gracious purpose for the fulfilment of which this world of time affords no adequate scope, but the glory of which will only be revealed in eternity.

It is a constant source of wonder to me that this priceless gem of Charles Wesley is so little known and so rarely sung in our churches. It cannot be because of the tune, which is pleasant and easy to learn. Perhaps one reason is the widespread popularity of Joseph Hart's short hymn with the lilting tune, 'This, this is the God we adore'. This hymn was written about the same time and contains some of the same ideas.

> *Whose love is as great as His power,*
> *And neither knows measure nor end.*

Also

> '*Tis Jesus, the first and the last,*
> *Whose Spirit shall guide us safe home.*

It is right that we should prize it and make full use of it, but Charles Wesley's hymn is fuller and richer, and I wish it could be learned by heart and become in frequent use among all our people, for it sums up better than anything else I know what I believe to be the Faith of a Methodist.

> *Jesus, the First and Last,*
> *On Thee my soul is cast:*
> *Thou didst Thy work begin*
> *By blotting out my sin;*
> *Thou wilt the root remove,*
> *And perfect me in love.*
>
> *Yet when the work is done,*
> *The work is but begun:*
> *Partaker of Thy grace,*
> *I long to see Thy face;*
> *The first I prove below,*
> *The last I die to know.*